Germ Wars

Battling Killer Bacteria and Microbes

ROSEN
PUBLISHING
New York

Published in 2008 by The Rosen Publishing Group, Inc.
29 East 21st Street, New York, NY 10010

The articles in this book first appeared in the pages of *Scientific American*, as follows: "Beyond Chicken Soup" by William A. Haseltine, November 2001; "Behind Enemy Lines" by K. C. Nicolaou and Christopher N. C. Boddy, May 2001; "Edible Vaccines" by William H. R. Langridge, Sidebar by Ricki Rusting, September 2000; "The Unmet Challenges of Hepatitis C" by Adrian M. Di Bisceglie and Bruce R. Bacon, October 1999; "Attacking Anthrax" by John A. T. Young and R. John Collier, March 2002; "Shoot This Deer" by Philip Yam, June 2003; "Hope in a Vial" by Carol Ezzell, June 2002.

First Edition

Library of Congress Cataloging-in-Publication Data

Germ wars: battling killer bacteria and microbes. — 1st ed.
   p. cm. — (Scientific American cutting-edge science)
"The articles in this book first appeared in the pages of Scientific American."
Includes index.
ISBN-13: 978-1-4042-1405-7 (library binding)
1. Medical microbiology—Popular works. 2. Microbiology—Popular works. 3. Microbiologists—Popular works. I. Scientific American.
QR46.G453 2008
616.9'041—dc22

                                                    2007038763

Manufactured in Singapore

Illustration credits: Cover (foreground) Jeff Johnson; Cover (background) Keith Kasnot; Source: Charles M. Rice Washington University School of Medicine; pp. 36, 51, 56 Jeff Johnson; p. 45 Jared Schneidman Design; pp. 64, 65, 74 Laurie Grace; pp. 72, 73 Keith Kasnot; Source: Charles M. Rice Washington University School of Medicine; pp. 88, 89 Bryan Christie Design; p. 113 Laurie Grace, Sources: Unaids (statistics) and Vadim Zalunin Los Alamos National Laboratory (clade Boundaries); p. 116 Terese Winslow.

On the cover: Illustrations of germs.

Table of Contents

Introduction

The human body has an impressive arsenal of defenses against pathogens. But bacteria and viruses are wily opponents, and tackling the most dangerous ones has become a battle of wits—one in which scientists have had both stunning successes and frustrating defeats. They must remain vigilant: germs have plagued our species since its inception and they are here to stay.

Scientific American has long covered developments in the war on germs. In this book, prominent researchers and journalists discuss the new weapons of this war, such as virus-fighting drugs, edible vaccines, and novel antibiotics; emerging enemies, such as anthrax and chronic wasting disease; and the all-too familiar foes HIV and hepatitis C. —***The Editors***

"Beyond
I.   Chicken Soup"

By William A. Haseltine

The antiviral era is upon us, with an array of virus-fighting drugs on the market and in development. Research into viral genomes is fueling much of this progress.

Back in the mid-1980s, when scientists first learned that a virus caused a relentless new disease named AIDS, pharmacy shelves were loaded with drugs able to treat bacterial infections. For viral diseases, though, medicine had little to offer beyond chicken soup and a cluster of vaccines. The story is dramatically different today. Dozens of antiviral therapies, including several new vaccines, are available, and hundreds more are in development. If the 1950s were the golden age of antibiotics, we are now in the early years of the golden age of antivirals.

This richness springs from various sources. Pharmaceutical companies would certainly point to the advent in the past 15 years of sophisticated techniques for discovering all manner of drugs. At the same time, frantic efforts to find lifesaving therapies for HIV, the cause of AIDS, have suggested creative ways to fight not only HIV but other viruses, too.

A little-recognized but more important force has also been at work: viral genomics, which deciphers the sequence of "letters," or nucleic acids, in a virus's genetic "text." This sequence includes the letters in all the virus's

genes, which form the blueprints for viral proteins;
these proteins, in turn, serve as the structural elements
and the working parts of the virus and thus control its
behavior. With a full or even a partial genome sequence
in hand, scientists can quickly learn many details of
how a virus causes disease—and which stages of the
process might be particularly vulnerable to attack. In
2001 the full genome of any virus can be sequenced
within days, making it possible to spot that virus's
weaknesses with unprecedented speed.

The majority of antivirals on sale these days take
aim at HIV, herpesviruses (responsible for a range of
ills, from cold sores to encephalitis), and hepatitis B
and C viruses (both of which can cause liver cancer).
HIV and these forms of hepatitis will surely remain a
main focus of investigation for some time; together
they cause more than 250,000 cases of disease in
the U.S. every year and millions in other countries.
Biologists, however, are working aggressively to
combat other viral illnesses as well. I cannot begin to
describe all the classes of antivirals on the market
and under study, but I do hope this article will offer
a sense of the extraordinary advances that genomics
and other sophisticated technologies have made
possible in recent years.

Drug-Search Strategies

The earliest antivirals (mainly against herpes) were
introduced in the 1960s and emerged from traditional

drug-discovery methods. Viruses are structurally simple, essentially consisting of genes and perhaps some enzymes (biological catalysts) encased in a protein capsule and sometimes also in a lipid envelope. Because this design requires viruses to replicate inside cells, investigators infected cells, grew them in culture and exposed the cultures to chemicals that might plausibly inhibit viral activities known at the time. Chemicals that reduced the amount of virus in the culture were considered for in-depth investigation. Beyond being a rather hit-or-miss process, such screening left scientists with few clues to other viral activities worth attacking. This handicap hampered efforts to develop drugs that were more effective or had fewer side effects.

Genomics has been a springboard for discovering fresh targets for attack and has thus opened the way to development of whole new classes of antiviral drugs. Most viral targets selected since the 1980s have been identified with the help of genomics, even though the term itself was only coined in the late 1980s, well after some of the currently available antiviral drugs were developed.

After investigators decipher the sequence of code letters in a given virus, they can enlist computers to compare that sequence with those already identified in other organisms, including other viruses, and thereby learn how the sequence is segmented into genes. Strings of code letters that closely resemble known genes in other organisms are likely to constitute genes in the virus as well and to give rise to proteins that have similar structures. Having located a virus's genes, scientists can study the functions of the corresponding proteins and thus build a comprehensive picture of the molecular steps by which the virus of interest gains a foothold and thrives in the body.

That picture, in turn, can highlight the proteins—and the domains within those proteins—that would be good to disable. In general, investigators favor targets whose disruption would impair viral activity most. They also like to focus on protein domains that bear little resemblance to those in humans, to avoid harming healthy cells and causing intolerable side effects. They take aim, too, at protein domains that are basically identical in all major strains of the virus, so that the drug will be useful against the broadest possible range of viral variants.

After researchers identify a viral target, they can enlist various techniques to find drugs that are able to perturb it. Drug sleuths can, for example, take advantage of standard genetic engineering (introduced in the 1970s) to produce pure copies of a selected protein for use in drug development. They insert the corresponding gene into bacteria or other types of cells, which synthesize endless copies of the encoded protein. The resulting protein molecules can then form the basis of rapid screening tests: only substances that bind to them are pursued further.

Alternatively, investigators might analyze the three-dimensional structure of a protein domain and then design drugs that bind tightly to that region.

For instance, they might construct a compound that inhibits the active site of an enzyme crucial to viral reproduction. Drugmakers can also combine old-fashioned screening methods with the newer methods based on structures.

Advanced approaches to drug discovery have generated ideas for thwarting viruses at all stages of their life cycles. Viral species vary in the fine details of their reproductive strategies. In general, though, the stages of viral replication include attachment to the cells of a host, release of viral genes into the cells' interiors, replication of all viral genes and proteins (with help from the cells' own protein-making machinery), joining of the components into hordes of viral particles, and escape of those particles to begin the cycle again in other cells.

The ideal time to ambush a virus is in the earliest stage of an infection, before it has had time to spread throughout the body and cause symptoms. Vaccines prove their worth at that point, because they prime a person's immune system to specifically destroy a chosen disease-causing agent, or pathogen, almost as soon as it enters the body. Historically vaccines have achieved this priming by exposing a person to a killed or weakened version of the infectious agent that cannot make enough copies of itself to cause disease. So-called subunit vaccines are the most common alternative to these. They contain mere fragments of a pathogen; fragments alone have no way to produce an infection but, if selected carefully, can evoke a protective immune response.

Overview/Antiviral Drugs

- Deciphering the genetic sequences, or genomes, of humans and of a variety of viruses has enabled scientists to devise drugs for diseases such as AIDS, hepatitis and influenza.
- After decoding the genetic sequence of a virus, researchers can use computers to compare its sequence with those of other viruses—a process known loosely as genomics. The comparison allows drugmakers to identify genes in the new virus that encode molecules worth targeting.
- Viruses have complex life cycles but are vulnerable to attack by pharmaceuticals at nearly every stage.

An early subunit vaccine, for hepatitis B, was made by isolating the virus from the plasma (the fluid component of blood) of people who were infected and then purifying the desired proteins. Today a subunit hepatitis B vaccine is made by genetic engineering. Scientists use the gene for a specific hepatitis B protein to manufacture pure copies of the protein. Additional vaccines developed with the help of genomics are in development for other important viral diseases, among them dengue fever, genital herpes and the often fatal hemorrhagic fever caused by the Ebola virus.

Several vaccines are being investigated for preventing or treating HIV. But HIV's genes mutate rapidly, giving rise to many viral strains; hence, a vaccine that induces a reaction against certain strains might have no effect against others. By comparing the genomes of the various HIV strains, researchers can find sequences that are present in most of them and then use those sequences to produce purified viral protein fragments. These can be tested for their ability to induce immune protection against strains found worldwide. Or vaccines might be tailored to the HIV variants prominent in particular regions.

Bar Entry

Treatments become important when a vaccine is not available or not effective. Antiviral treatments effect cures for some patients, but so far most of them tend to reduce the severity or duration of a viral infection. One group of therapies limits viral activity by interfering with entry into a favored cell type.

The term "entry" actually covers a few steps, beginning with the binding of the virus to some docking site, or receptor, on a host cell and ending with "uncoating" inside the cell; during uncoating, the protein capsule (capsid) breaks up, releasing the virus's genes. Entry for enveloped viruses requires an extra step. Before uncoating can occur, these microorganisms must fuse their envelope with the cell membrane or with the membrane of a vesicle that draws the virus into the cell's interior.

Several entry-inhibiting drugs in development attempt to block HIV from penetrating cells. Close examination of the way HIV interacts with its favorite hosts (white blood cells called helper T cells) has indicated that it docks with molecules on those cells called CD4 and CCR5. Although blocking CD4 has failed to prevent HIV from entering cells, blocking CCR5 may yet do so.

Amantidine and rimantidine, the first two (of four) influenza drugs to be introduced, interrupt other parts of the entry process. Drugmakers found the compounds by screening likely chemicals for their overall ability to interfere with viral replication, but they have since learned more specifically that the compounds probably act by inhibiting fusion and uncoating. Fusion inhibitors discovered with the aid of genomic information are also being pursued against respiratory syncytial virus (a cause of lung disease in infants born prematurely), hepatitis B and C, and HIV.

Many colds could soon be controlled by another entry blocker, pleconaril, which is reportedly close to receiving federal approval. Genomic and structural comparisons have shown that a pocket on the surface of rhinoviruses (responsible for most colds) is similar in most variants. Pleconaril binds to this pocket in a way that inhibits the uncoating of the virus. The drug also appears to be active against enteroviruses, which can cause diarrhea, meningitis, conjunctivitis and encephalitis.

Jam the Copier

A number of antivirals on sale and under study operate after uncoating, when the viral genome, which can take the form of DNA or RNA, is freed for copying and directing the production of viral proteins. Several of the agents that inhibit genome replication are nucleoside or nucleotide analogues, which resemble the building blocks of genes. The enzymes that copy viral DNA or RNA incorporate these mimics into the nascent strands. Then the mimics prevent the enzyme from adding any further building blocks, effectively aborting viral replication.

Acyclovir, the earliest antiviral proved to be both effective and relatively nontoxic, is a nucleoside analogue that was discovered by screening selected compounds for their ability to interfere with the replication of herpes simplex virus. It is prescribed mainly for genital herpes, but chemical relatives have value against other herpesvirus infections, such as shingles caused by varicella zoster and inflammation of the retina caused by cytomegalovirus.

The first drug approved for use against HIV, zidovudine (AZT), is a nucleoside analogue as well. Initially developed as an anticancer drug, it was shown to interfere with the activity of reverse transcriptase, an enzyme that HIV uses to copy its RNA genome into DNA. If this copying step is successful, other HIV enzymes splice the DNA into the chromosomes of an invaded cell, where the integrated DNA directs viral reproduction.

AZT can cause severe side effects, such as anemia. But studies of reverse transcriptase, informed by knowledge of the enzyme's gene sequence, have enabled drug developers to introduce less toxic nucleoside analogues. One of these, lamivudine, has also been approved for hepatitis B, which uses reverse transcriptase to convert RNA copies of its DNA genome back into DNA. Intense analyses of HIV reverse transcriptase have led as well to improved versions of a class of reverse transcriptase inhibitors that do not resemble nucleosides.

Genomics has uncovered additional targets that could be hit to interrupt replication of the HIV genome. Among these is RNase H, a part of reverse transcriptase that separates freshly minted HIV DNA from RNA. Another is the active site of integrase, an enzyme that splices DNA into the chromosomal DNA of the infected cell. An integrase inhibitor is now being tested in HIV-infected volunteers.

Impede Protein Production

All viruses must at some point in their life cycle transcribe genes into mobile strands of messenger RNA, which the host cell then "translates," or uses as a guide for making the encoded proteins. Several drugs in development interfere with the transcription stage by preventing proteins known as transcription factors from attaching to viral DNA and switching on the production of messenger RNA.

Genomics helped to identify the targets for many of these agents. It also made possible a novel kind of drug: the antisense molecule. If genomic research shows that a particular protein is needed by a virus, workers can halt the protein's production by masking part of the corresponding RNA template with a custom-designed DNA fragment able to bind firmly to the selected RNA sequence. An antisense drug, fomivirsen, is already used to treat eye infections caused by cytomegalovirus in AIDS patients. And antisense agents are in development for other viral diseases; one of them blocks production of the HIV protein Tat, which is needed for the transcription of other HIV genes.

Drugmakers have also used their knowledge of viral genomes to identify sites in viral RNA that are susceptible to cutting by ribozymes—enzymatic forms of RNA. A ribozyme is being tested in patients with hepatitis C, and ribozymes for HIV are in earlier stages of development. Some such projects employ gene therapy: specially designed genes are introduced into cells, which then produce the needed ribozymes. Other types of HIV gene therapy under study give rise to specialized antibodies that seek targets inside infected cells or to other proteins that latch onto certain viral gene sequences within those cells.

Some viruses produce a protein chain in a cell that must be spliced to yield functional proteins. HIV is among them, and an enzyme known as a protease performs this cutting. When analyses of the HIV genome pinpointed this activity, scientists began to consider the protease a drug target. With enormous help from computer-assisted structure-based research, potent

Antiviral Drugs Today

Sampling of antiviral drugs on the market appears below. Many owe their existence, at least in part, to viral genomics. About 30 other viral drugs based on an understanding of viral genomics are in human tests.

DRUG NAMES	SPECIFIC ROLES	MAIN VIRAL DISEASES TARGETED
DISRUPTORS OF GENOME		
abacavir, didanosine, stavudine, zalcitabine, zidovudine	Nucleoside analogue inhibitors of reverse transcriptase	HIV infection
acyclovir, ganciclovir, penciclovir	Nucleoside analogue inhibitors of the enzyme that duplicates viral DNA	Herpes infections; retinal inflammation caused by cytomegalovirus
cidofovir	Nucleotide analogue inhibitor of the enzyme that duplicates viral DNA	Retinal inflammation caused by cytomegalovirus
delavardine, efavirenz	Nonnucleoside, nonnucleotide inhibitors of reverse transcriptase	HIV infection
lamivudine	Nucleoside analogue inhibitor of reverse transcriptase	HIV, hepatitis B infections
ribavirin	Synthetic nucleoside that induces mutations in viral genes	Hepatitis C infection
DISRUPTORS OF PROTEIN SYNTHESIS		
amprenavir, indinavir, lopinavir, nelfinavir, ritonavir, saquinavir	Inhibitors of HIV protease	HIV infection
fomivirsen	Antisense molecule that blocks translation of viral RNA	Retinal inflammation caused by cytomegalovirus
interferon alpha	Activator of intracellular immune defenses that block viral protein synthesis	Hepatitis B and C infections
BLOCKERS OF VIRAL SPREAD FROM CELL TO CELL		
oseltamivir, zanamivir	Inhibitors of viral release	Influenza
palivizumab	Humanized monoclonal antibody that marks virus for destruction	Respiratory syncytial infection

protease inhibitors became available in the 1990s, and more are in development. The inhibitors that are available so far can cause disturbing side effects, such as the accumulation of fat in unusual places, but they nonetheless prolong overall health and life in many people when taken in combination with other HIV antivirals. A new generation of protease inhibitors is in the research pipeline.

Stop Traffic

Even if viral genomes and proteins are reproduced in a cell, they will be harmless unless they form new viral particles able to escape from the cell and migrate to other cells. The most recent influenza drugs, zanamivir and oseltamivir, act at this stage. A molecule called neuraminidase, which is found on the surface of both major types of influenza (A and B), has long been known to play a role in helping viral particles escape from the cells that produced them. Genomic comparisons revealed that the active site of neuraminidase is similar among various influenza strains, and structural studies enabled researchers to design compounds able to plug that site. The other flu drugs act only against type A.

Drugs can prevent the cell-to-cell spread of viruses in a different way—by augmenting a patient's immune responses. Some of these responses are nonspecific: the drugs may restrain the spread through the body of various kinds of invaders rather than homing in on a particular pathogen. Molecules called interferons take part in this type of immunity, inhibiting protein synthesis and other aspects of viral replication in infected cells. For that reason, one form of human interferon, interferon alpha, has been a mainstay of therapy for hepatitis B and C. (For hepatitis C, it is used with an older drug, ribavirin.) Other interferons are under study, too.

More specific immune responses include the production of standard antibodies, which recognize some fragment of a protein on the surface of a viral invader, bind to that protein and mark the virus for destruction by other parts of the immune system. Once researchers have the gene sequence encoding a viral surface protein, they can generate pure, or "monoclonal," antibodies to selected regions of the protein. One monoclonal is on the market for preventing respiratory syncytial virus in babies at risk for this infection; another is being tested in patients suffering from hepatitis B.

Comparisons of viral and human genomes have suggested yet another antiviral strategy. A number of viruses, it turns out, produce proteins that resemble molecules involved in the immune response. Moreover, certain of those viral mimics disrupt the immune onslaught and thus help the virus to evade destruction. Drugs able to intercept such evasion-enabling proteins may preserve full immune responses and speed the organism's recovery from numerous viral diseases. The hunt for such agents is under way.

The Resistance Demon

The pace of antiviral drug discovery is nothing short of breathtaking, but at the same time, drugmakers have to confront a hard reality: viruses are very likely to develop resistance, or insensitivity, to many drugs. Resistance is especially probable when the compounds are used for long periods, as they are in such chronic diseases as HIV and in quite a few cases of hepatitis B and C. Indeed, for every HIV drug in the present arsenal, some viral strain exists that is resistant to it and, often, to additional drugs. This resistance stems from the tendency of viruses—especially RNA viruses and most especially HIV—to mutate rapidly. When a mutation enables a viral strain to overcome some obstacle to reproduction (such as a drug), that strain will thrive in the face of the obstacle.

To keep the resistance demon at bay until effective vaccines are found, pharmaceutical companies will have to develop more drugs. When mutants resistant to a particular drug arise, reading their genetic text can indicate where the mutation lies in the viral genome and suggest how that mutation might alter the interaction between the affected viral protein and the drug. Armed with that information, researchers can begin structure-based or other studies designed to keep the drug working despite the mutation.

Pharmaceutical developers are also selecting novel drugs based on their ability to combat viral strains that are resistant to other drugs. Recently, for instance, DuPont Pharmaceuticals chose a new HIV nonnucleoside reverse transcriptase inhibitor, DPC 083, for development precisely because of its ability to overcome viral resistance to such inhibitors. The company's researchers first examined the mutations in the reverse transcriptase gene that conferred resistance. Next they turned to computer modeling to find drug designs likely to inhibit the reverse transcriptase enzyme in spite of those mutations. Then, using genetic engineering, they created viruses that produced the mutant enzymes and selected the compound best able to limit reproduction

Deciphered Viruses

Some medically important viruses whose genomes have been sequenced are listed below. Frederick Sanger of the University of Cambridge and his colleagues determined the DNA sequence of the first viral genome—from a virus that infects bacteria—in 1977.

VIRUS	DISEASE	YEAR SEQUENCED
Human poliovirus	Poliomyelitis	1981
Influenza A virus	Influenza	1981
Hepatitis B virus	Hepatitis B	1984
Human rhinovirus type 14	Common cold	1984
HIV-1	AIDS	1985
Human papillomavirus type 16	Cervical cancer	1985
Dengue virus type 1	Dengue fever	1987
Hepatitis A virus	Hepatitis A	1987
Herpes simplex virus type 1	Cold sores	1988
Hepatitis C virus	Hepatitis C	1990
Cytomegalovirus	Retinal infections in HIV-infected people	1991
Variola virus	Smallpox	1992
Ebola virus	Ebola hemorrhagic fever	1993
Respiratory syncytial virus	Childhood respiratory infections	1996
Human parainfluenza virus 3	Childhood respiratory infections	1998

by those viruses. The drug is now being evaluated in HIV-infected patients.

It may be some time before virtually all serious viral infections are either preventable by vaccines or treatable by some effective drug therapy. But now that the sequence of the human genome is available in draft form, drug designers will identify a number of previously undiscovered proteins that stimulate the production of antiviral antibodies or that energize other parts of the immune system against viruses. I fully expect these discoveries to translate into yet more antivirals. The insights gleaned from the human genome, viral genomes and other advanced drug-discovery methods are sure to provide a flood of needed antivirals within the next 10 to 20 years.

More to Explore

Viral Strategies of Immune Evasion. Hidde L. Ploegh in *Science*, Vol. 280, No. 5361, pages 248–253; April 10, 1998.

Strategies for Antiviral Drug Discovery. Philip S. Jones in *Antiviral Chemistry and Chemotherapy*, Vol. 9, No. 4, pages 283–302; July 1998.

New Technologies for Making Vaccines. Ronald W. Ellis in *Vaccine*, Vol. 17, No. 13-14, pages 1596–1604; March 26, 1999.

Protein Design of an HIV-1 Entry Inhibitor. Michael J. Root, Michael S. Kay and Peter S. Kim in *Science*, Vol. 291, No. 5505, pages 884–888; February 2, 2001.

Antiviral Chemotherapy: General Overview. Jack M. Bernstein, Wright State University School of Medicine, Division of Infectious Diseases, 2000. Available at **www.med.wright.edu/im/ AntiviralChemotherapy.html.**

About the Author

WILLIAM A. HASELTINE, who has a doctorate in biophysics from Harvard University, is the chairman of the board of directors and chief executive officer of Human Genome Sciences; he is also editor in chief of a new publication, the *Journal of Regenerative Medicine,* and serves on the editorial boards of several other scientific journals. He was a professor at the Dana-Farber Cancer Institute, an affiliate of Harvard Medical School, and at the Harvard School of Public Health from 1988 to 1995. His laboratory was the first to assemble the sequence of the AIDS virus genome. Since 1981 he has helped found more than 20 biotechnology companies.

"Behind
2. Enemy Lines"

By K. C. Nicolaou and Christopher N. C. Boddy

A close look at the inner workings of microbes in this era of escalating antibiotic resistance is offering new strategies for designing drugs.

In the celebrated movie *Crouching Tiger, Hidden Dragon*, two warriors face each other in a closed courtyard whose walls are lined with a fantastic array of martial-arts weaponry, including iron rods, knives, spears and swords.

The older, more experienced warrior grabs one instrument after another from the arsenal and battles energetically and fluidly with them. But one after another, the weapons prove useless. Each, in turn, is broken or thrown aside, the shards of an era that can hold little contest against a young, triumphant, upstart warrior who has learned not only the old ways but some that are new.

One of the foundations of the modern medical system is being similarly overcome. Health care workers are increasingly finding that nearly every weapon in their arsenal of more than 150 antibiotics is becoming useless. Bacteria that have survived attack by antibiotics have learned from the enemy and have grown stronger; some that have not had skirmishes themselves have learned from others that have. The result is a rising number of antibiotic-resistant strains. Infections—including tuberculosis, meningitis and pneumonia—that would once have been easily treated with an antibiotic are no longer so readily thwarted. More and more bacterial infections are proving deadly.

Bacteria are wily warriors, but even so, we have given them—and continue to give them—exactly what they need for their stunning success. By misusing and overusing antibiotics, we have encouraged super-races of bacteria to evolve. We don't finish a course of antibiotics. Or we use them for viral and other inappropriate infections—in fact, researchers estimate that one third to one half of all antibiotic prescriptions are unnecessary. We put 70 percent of the antibiotics we produce in the U.S. each year into our livestock. We add antibiotics to our dishwashing liquid and our hand soap. In all these ways, we encourage the weak to die and the strong to become stronger [see "The Challenge of Antibiotic Resistance," by Stuart B. Levy; *Scientific American*, March 1998].

Yet even absent the massive societal and medical misuse of these medications, the unavoidable destiny of any antibiotic is obsolescence. Bacteria—which grow quickly through many cell divisions a day—will always learn something new; some of the strongest will always survive and thrive. So we have had to become ever more wily ourselves.

In the past 10 years, long-standing complacency about vanquishing infection has been replaced by a dramatic increase in antibacterial research in academic, government and industrial laboratories. Scientists the world over are finding imaginative strategies to attack bacteria. Although they will have a limited life span, new antibiotics are being developed using information gleaned from genome and protein studies. This exciting research and drug development is no panacea, but if combined with the responsible use of antibiotics, it can offer some hope. Indeed, in April 2000 the Food and Drug Administration approved the first new kind of clinical antibiotic in 35 years—linezolid—and several agents are already in the pharmaceutical pipeline.

Dismantling the Wall

Almost all the antibiotics that have been developed so far have come from nature. Scientists have identified them and improved on them, but they certainly did not invent them. Since the beginning of life on this planet, organisms have fought over limited resources. These battles resulted in the evolution of antibiotics. The ability to produce such powerful compounds gives an organism—a fungus or plant or even another species of bacteria—an advantage over bacteria susceptible to the antibiotic. This selective pressure is the force driving the development of antibiotics in nature.

Our window onto this biological arms race first opened with the discovery of penicillin in 1928. Alexander Fleming of St. Mary's Hospital Medical School at London University noticed that the

MCNEEL MIDDLE SCHOOL
BELOIT, WISCONSIN 53511

mold *Penicillium notatum* was able to kill nearby *Staphylococcus* bacteria growing in agar in a petri dish. Thus was the field of antibiotics born. By randomly testing compounds, such as other molds, to see if they could kill bacteria or retard their growth, later researchers were able to identify a whole suite of antibiotics.

One of the most successful of these has been vancomycin, first identified by Eli Lilly and Company in 1956. Understanding how it works—a feat that has taken three decades to accomplish—has allowed us insight into the mechanism behind a class of antibiotics called the glycopeptides, one of the seven or so major kinds of antibiotics. This insight is proving important because vancomycin has become the antibiotic of last resort, the only remaining drug effective against the most deadly of all hospital-acquired infections: methicillin-resistant *Staphylococcus aureus*. And yet vancomycin's power—like that of the great, experienced warrior—is itself in jeopardy.

Vancomycin works by targeting the bacterial cell wall, which surrounds the cell and its membrane, imparting structure and support. Because human and other mammalian cells lack such a wall (instead their cells are held up by an internal structure called a cytoskeleton), vancomycin and related drugs are not dangerous to them. This bacterial wall is composed mostly of peptidoglycan, a material that contains both peptides and sugars (hence its name). As the cell assembles this material—a constant process, because old peptidoglycan needs to be replaced as it breaks down—sugar units are linked together by an enzyme called transglycosidase to form a structural core. Every other sugar unit along this core has a short peptide chain attached to it. Each peptide chain is composed of five amino acids, the last three being an L-lysine and two D-alanines. An enzyme called transpeptidase then hooks these peptide chains together, removing the final D-alanine and attaching the penultimate D-alanine to an L-lysine from a different sugar chain. As a result, the sugar chains are crocheted together through their peptide chains. All this linking and cross-linking creates a thickly woven material essential for the cell's survival: without it, the cell would burst from its own internal pressure.

Vancomycin meddles in the formation of this essential material. The antibiotic is perfectly suited to bind to the peptide chains before they are linked to one another by transpeptidase. The drug fastens onto the terminal D-alanines, preventing the enzyme from doing its work. Without the thicket of cross-linking connections, peptidoglycan becomes weak, like an ill-woven fabric. The cell wall rends, and cell death rapidly occurs.

Resisting Resistance

Vancomycin's lovely fit at the end of the peptide chain is the key to its effectiveness as an antibiotic. Unfortunately, its peptide connection is also the key to resistance on the part of bacteria. In 1998 vancomycin-resistant *S. aureus* emerged in three geographic locations. Physicians and hospital workers are increasingly worried that these strains will become widespread, leaving them with no treatment for lethal staph infections.

Understanding resistance offers the possibility of overcoming it, and so scientists have focused on another bacterium that has been known to be resistant to the powerful drug since the late 1980s: vancomycin-resistant enterococci (VRE). In most enterococci bacteria, vancomycin does what it does best: it binds to the terminal two D-alanines. At a molecular level, this binding entails five hydrogen bonds—think of them as five fingers clasping a ball. But in VRE, the peptide chain is slightly different. Its final D-alanine is altered by a simple substitution: an oxygen replaces a pair of atoms consisting of a nitrogen bonded to a hydrogen. In molecular terms, this one substitution means that vancomycin can bind to the peptide chain with only four hydrogen bonds. The loss of that one bond makes all the difference. With only four fingers grasping the ball, the drug cannot hold on as well, and enzymes pry it off, allowing the peptide chains to link up and the peptidoglycan to become tightly woven once again. One atomic substitution reduces the drug's activity by a factor of 1,000.

Researchers have turned to other members of the glycopeptide class of antibiotics to see if some have a strategy that vancomycin could adopt against VRE. It turns out that some members of the group have long, hydrophobic—that is, oily—chains attached to them that have proved useful. These chains prefer to be surrounded by other hydrophobic molecules, such as those that make up the cell membrane, which is hidden behind the protective peptidoglycan shield. Researchers at Eli Lilly have borrowed this idea and attached hydrophobic chains to vancomycin, creating an analogue called LY333328. The drug connects to the cell membrane in high concentrations, allowing it more purchase and, as a consequence, more power against peptidoglycan. This analogue is effective against VRE and is now in clinical trials.

Other glycopeptide antibiotics use a different strategy: dimerization. This process occurs when two molecules bind to each other to form a single complex. By creating couples, or dimers, of vancomycin, researchers can enhance the drug's strength. One vancomycin binds to peptidoglycan, bringing the other half of the pair—the other molecule of vancomycin— into proximity as well. The drug is more effective because more of it is present. One of the aims of our laboratory is to alter vancomycin so it pairs up more readily, and we have recently developed a number of dimeric vancomycin molecules with exceptional activity against VRE.

Even so, the good news may be short-lived. A second mechanism by which VRE foils vancomycin has recently been discovered. Rather than substituting an atom in the final D-alanine, the bacterium adds an amino acid that is much larger than D-alanine to the very end of the peptide chain. Like a muscular bouncer blocking a doorway, the amino acid prevents vancomycin from reaching its destination.

One method by which the deadly *S. aureus* gains resistance is becoming clear as well. The bacterium thickens the peptidoglycan layer but simultaneously reduces the linking between the peptide fragments. So it makes no difference if vancomycin binds to D-alanine: thickness has replaced interweaving as the source of the peptidoglycan's strength. Vancomycin's meddling has no effect.

The Cutting Edge

As the story of vancomycin shows, tiny molecular alterations can make all the difference, and bacteria find myriad strategies to outwit drugs. Obviously, the need for new, improved or even revived antibiotics is enormous. Historically, the drug discovery process identified candidates using whole-cell screening, in which molecules of interest were applied to living bacterial cells. This approach has been very successful and underlies the discovery of many drugs, including vancomycin. Its advantage lies in its simplicity and in the fact that every possible drug target in the cell is screened. But screening such a large number of targets also has a drawback. Various targets are shared by both bacteria and humans; compounds that act against those are toxic to people. Furthermore, researchers gain no information about the mechanism of action: chemists know that an agent worked, but they have no information about how. Without this critical information it is virtually impossible to bring a new drug all the way to the clinic.

Molecular-level assays provide a powerful alternative. This form of screen identifies only those compounds that have a specified mechanism of action. For instance, one such screen would look specifically for inhibitors of the transpeptidase enzyme. Although these assays are difficult to design, they yield potential drugs with known modes of action. The trouble is that only one enzyme is usually investigated at a time. It would be a vast improvement in the drug discovery process if researchers could review more than one target simul-taneously, as they do in the whole-cell process, but also retain the implicit knowledge of the way the drug works. Scientists have accomplished this feat by figuring out how to assemble the many-enzyme pathway of a certain bacterium in a test tube. Using this system, they can identify molecules that either strongly disrupt one of the enzymes or subtly disrupt many of them.

Automation and miniaturization have also signifi-cantly improved the rate at which compounds can be screened. Robotics in so-called high-throughput machines allow scientists to review thousands of compounds per week. At the same time, miniaturization has cut the cost of the process by using ever smaller amounts of reagents. In the new ultrahigh-throughput screening systems, hundreds of thousands of compounds can be looked at cost-effectively in a single day. Accordingly, chemists have to work hard to keep up with the demand for molecules. Their work is made possible by new methods in combinatorial chemistry, which allows them to design huge libraries of compounds quickly [see "Combinatorial Chemistry and New Drugs," by Matthew J. Plunkett and Jonathan A. Ellman; *Scientific American*, April 1997]. In the future, some of these new molecules will most likely come from bacteria themselves. By understanding the way these organisms produce antibiotics, scientists can genetically engineer them to produce new related molecules.

The Genomic Advantage

The methodology of drug design and screening has benefited tremendously from recent developments in genomics. Information about genes and the synthesis of their proteins has allowed geneticists and chemists to go behind enemy lines and use inside information against the organism itself. This microbial counter-intelligence is taking place on several fronts, from sabotaging centrally important genes to putting a wrench in the production of a single protein and disrupting a bacterium's ability to infect an organism or to develop resistance.

Studies have revealed that many of the known targets of antibiotics are essential genes, genes that cause cell death if they are not functioning smoothly.

New genetic techniques are making the identification of these essential genes much faster. For instance, researchers are systematically analyzing all 6,000 or so genes of the yeast *Saccharomyces cerevisiae* for essential genes. Every gene can be experimentally disrupted and its effect on yeast determined. This effort will ultimately catalogue all the essential genes and will also provide insight into the action of other genes that could serve as targets for new antibiotics.

The proteins encoded by essential genes are not the only molecular-level targets that can lead to antibiotics. Genes that encode for virulence factors are also important. Virulence factors circumvent the host's immune response, allowing bacteria to colonize. In the past, it has been quite hard to identify these genes because they are "turned on," or transcribed, by events in the host's tissue that are very difficult to reproduce in the laboratory. Now a technique called in vivo expression technology (IVET) can insert a unique sequence of DNA, a form of tag that deactivates a gene, into each bacterial gene. Tagged bacteria are then used to infect an organism. The bacteria are later recovered and the tags identified. The disappearance of any tags means that the genes they were attached to were essential for the bacteria's survival—so essential that the bacteria could not survive in the host without the use of those genes.

Investigators have long hoped that by identifying and inhibiting these virulence factors, they can allow the body's immune system to combat pathogenic bacteria before they gain a foothold. And it seems that the hypothesis is bearing fruit. In a recent study, an experimental molecule that inhibited a virulence factor of the dangerous *S. aureus* permitted infected mice to resist and overcome infection.

In addition to identifying essential genes and virulence factors, researchers are discovering which genes confer antibiotic resistance. Targeting them provides a method to rejuvenate previously ineffective antibiotics. This is an approach used with ß-lactum antibiotics such as penicillin. The most common mechanism of resistance to ß-lactam antibiotics is the bacterial production of an enzyme called ß-lactamase, which breaks one of the antibiotic's chemical bonds, changing its structure and preventing it from inhibiting the enzyme transpeptidase. If ß-lactamase is silenced, the antibiotics remain useful. A ß-lactamase inhibitor called clavulanic acid does just that and is mixed with amoxicillin to create an antibiotic marketed as Augmentin.

In the near future, with improvements in the field of DNA transcriptional profiling, it will become routine to identify resistance determinants, such as ß-lactamase, and virulence factors. Such profiling allows scientists to identify all the genes that are in use under different growth conditions in the cell. Virulence genes can be determined by identifying bacterial genes whose expression increases on infecting a host. Genes that code for antibiotic resistance can be determined by comparing expression levels in bacteria treated with the antibiotic and those not treated. Though still in its infancy, this technique monitored tiny changes in the number of transcription events. With DNA transcriptional profiling, researchers should also be able to determine whether certain drugs have entirely new mechanisms of action or cellular targets that could open up new fields of antibiotic research.

Killing the Messenger

Another interesting line of genomic research entails interfering with bacterial RNA. Most RNA is ribosomal RNA (rRNA), which forms a major structural component of ribosomes, the cellular factories where proteins are assembled. Ribosomal RNA is vulnerable because it has various places where drugs can attach and because it lacks the ability to repair itself. In 1987 scientists determined that antibiotics in the aminoglycoside group—which includes streptomycin—bind to rRNA, causing the ribosome to misread the genetic code for protein assembly. Many of these antibiotics, however, are toxic and have only limited usefulness. Recently scientists at the Scripps Research Institute in La Jolla, Calif., have reported a new synthetic aminoglycoside dimer that may have less toxicity.

Investigators can also interfere with messenger RNA (mRNA), which directs the assembly of proteins and travels between the genetic code and the ribosome. Messenger RNA is created by reading one strand of the DNA, using the same nucleic acid, or base pair, interactions that hold the double helix together. The

Antibiotics at Work

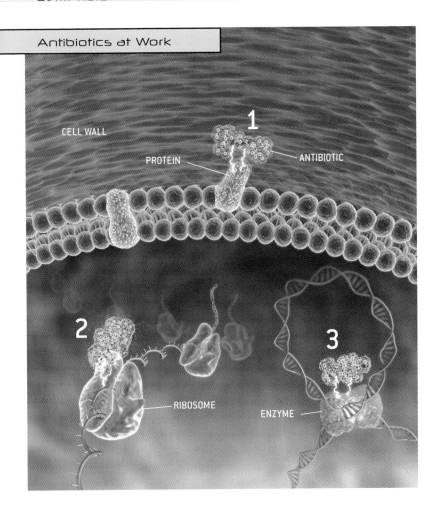

CELL WALL

PROTEIN

ANTIBIOTIC

1

2

RIBOSOME

ENZYME

3

Existing antibiotics fight infections by preventing bacteria from making essential substances. Vancomycin and ß-lactam antibiotics interfere with synthesis of the cell wall (1). Erythromycin and tetracycline disrupt ribosomes that make proteins (2). Quinolone antibiotics inhibit enzymes involved in replicating DNA (3), and sulfonamide antibiotics also interfere with DNA synthesis (not shown).

mRNA molecule then carries its message to the ribosome, where a protein is assembled through the process of translation. Because each mRNA codes for a specific protein and is distinct from other mRNAs, researchers have the opportunity to create interactions between small organic molecules—that is, not proteins—and specific mRNAs. Parke-Davis chemists have been able to use such an approach to combat HIV infection. They identified molecules that bind to a part of an mRNA sequence and prevent it from interacting with a required protein activator, thus inhibiting the replication of HIV. This proof-of-principle experiment should help pave the way for further studies of mRNA as a drug development target.

Scientific interest has been intense in another approach, called antisense therapy. By generating sequences of nucleotides that bind perfectly with a specific mRNA sequence, investigators can essentially straitjacket the mRNA. It cannot free itself from the drug, which either destroys it or inhibits it from acting. Although the FDA has recently approved the first antisense drug to treat human cytomegalovirus infections, antisense for bacterial infections has not succeeded yet for several reasons, including toxicity and the challenge of getting enough of the drug to the right spot. Nevertheless, the approach holds promise.

As is clear, all these genomic insights are making it possible to identify and evaluate a range of new biological targets against which chemists can direct their small, bulletlike molecules. A number of antibiotics developed in the past century cannot be used, because they harm us. But by comparing a potential target's genetic sequence with the genes found in humans, researchers can identify genes that are unique to bacteria and can focus on those. Similarly, by comparing a target's genetic sequence to those of other bacteria, they are able to evaluate the selectivity of a drug that would be generated from it. A target sequence that appears in all bacteria would very likely generate an antibiotic active against many different bacteria: a broad-spectrum antibiotic. In contrast, a target sequence that appears in only a few bacterial genomes would generate a narrow-spectrum antibiotic.

If physicians can identify early on which strain is causing an infection, they can hone their prescription to a narrow-spectrum antibiotic. Because this drug would affect only a subset of the bacterial population, selective pressure for the development of resistance would be reduced. Advances in the high-speed replication of DNA and transcriptional profiling may soon make identification of bacterial strains a routine medical procedure.

Although the picture looks brighter than it has for several decades, it is crucial that we recognize that the biological arms race is an ancient one. For every creative counterattack we make, bacteria will respond in kind— changing perhaps one atom in one amino acid. There will always be young warriors to challenge the old ones.

The hope is that we exercise restraint and that we use our ever expanding arsenal of weapons responsibly, not relegating them so quickly to obsolescence.

More to Explore

The Coming Plague: Newly Emerging Diseases in a World out of Balance. Laurie Garrett. Penguin USA, 1995.

The Chemistry, Biology, and Medicine of the Glycopeptide Antibiotics. K. C. Nicolaou, Christopher N. C. Boddy, Stefan Bräse and Nicolas Winssinger in *Angewandte Chemie International Edition*, Vol. 38, No. 15, pages 2096–2152; August 2, 1999.

Genome Prospecting. Barbara R. Jasny and Pamela J. Hines in *Science*, Vol. 286, pages 443–491; October 15, 1999.

About the Authors

K. C. NICOLAOU and *CHRISTOPHER N. C. BODDY* have worked together at the Scripps Research Institute in La Jolla, Calif., where Nicolaou is chairman of the department of chemistry and Boddy recently received his Ph.D. Nicolaou holds the Darlene Shiley Chair in Chemistry, the Aline W. and L. S. Skaggs Professorship in Chemical Biology and a professorship at the University of California, San Diego. His work in chemistry, biology and medicine has been described in more than 500 publications and 50 patents. Boddy's research has focused on the synthesis of vancomycin. He will soon be moving to Stanford University, where as a postdoctoral fellow he will continue work on antibiotics and anticancer agents. The authors are indebted to Nicolas Winssinger and Joshua Gruber for valuable discussions and assistance in preparing this article.

3. "Edible Vaccines"

By William H. R. Langridge

One day children may get immunized by munching on foods instead of enduring shots. More important, food vaccines might save millions who now die for lack of access to traditional inoculants.

Vaccines have accomplished near miracles in the fight against infectious disease. They have consigned smallpox to history and should soon do the same for polio. By the late 1990s an international campaign to immunize all the world's children against six devastating diseases was reportedly reaching 80 percent of infants (up from about 5 percent in the mid-1970s) and was reducing the annual death toll from those infections by roughly three million.

Yet these victories mask tragic gaps in delivery. The 20 percent of infants still missed by the six vaccines—against diphtheria, pertussis (whooping cough), polio, measles, tetanus and tuberculosis—account for about two million unnecessary deaths each year, especially in the most remote and impoverished parts of the globe. Upheavals in many developing nations now threaten to erode the advances of the recent past, and millions still die from infectious diseases for which immunizations are nonexistent, unreliable or too costly.

This situation is worrisome not only for the places that lack health care but for the entire world. Regions harboring infections that have faded from other areas are like bombs ready to explode. When environmental or social disasters undermine sanitation systems or displace communities—bringing people with little immunity into contact with carriers—infections that have been long gone from a population can come roaring back. Further, as international travel and trade make the earth a smaller place, diseases that arise in one locale are increasingly popping up continents away. Until everyone has routine access to vaccines, no one will be entirely safe.

In the early 1990s Charles J. Arntzen, then at Texas A&M University, conceived of a way to solve many of the problems that bar vaccines from reaching all too many children in developing nations. Soon after learning of a World Health Organization call for inexpensive, oral vaccines that needed no refrigeration, Arntzen visited Bangkok, where he saw a mother soothe a crying baby by offering a piece of banana. Plant biologists had already devised ways of introducing selected genes (the blueprints for proteins) into plants and inducing the altered, or "transgenic," plants to manufacture the encoded proteins. Perhaps, he mused, food could be genetically engineered to produce vaccines in their edible parts, which could then be eaten when inoculations were needed.

The advantages would be enormous. The plants could be grown locally, and cheaply, using the standard growing methods of a given region. Because many food plants can be regenerated readily, the crops could potentially be produced indefinitely without the growers having to purchase more seeds or plants year after year. Homegrown vaccines would also avoid the logistical and economic problems posed by having to transport traditional preparations over long distances, keeping them cold en route and at their destination. And, being edible, the vaccines would require no syringes—which, aside from costing something, can lead to infections if they become contaminated.

Efforts to make Arntzen's inspired vision a reality are still quite preliminary. Yet studies carried out in animals over the past 10 years, and small tests in people, encourage hope that edible vaccines can work. The research has also fueled speculation that certain food vaccines might help suppress autoimmunity—in which the body's defenses mistakenly attack normal, uninfected tissues. Among the autoimmune disorders that might be prevented or eased are type I diabetes (the kind that commonly arises during childhood), multiple sclerosis and rheumatoid arthritis.

By Any Other Name . . .

Regardless of how vaccines for infectious diseases are delivered, they all have the same aim: priming the immune system to swiftly destroy specific disease-causing agents, or pathogens, before the agents can multiply enough to cause symptoms. Classically, this priming has been achieved by presenting the immune system with whole viruses or bacteria that have been killed or made too weak to proliferate much.

On detecting the presence of a foreign organism in a vaccine, the immune system behaves as if the body were under attack by a fully potent antagonist. It mobilizes its various forces to root out and destroy the apparent invader—targeting the campaign to specific antigens (proteins recognized as foreign). The acute response soon abates, but it leaves behind sentries, known as "memory" cells, that remain on alert, ready to unleash whole armies of defenders if the real pathogen ever finds its way into the body. Some vaccines provide lifelong protection; others (such as those for cholera and tetanus) must be readministered periodically.

Classic vaccines pose a small but troubling risk that the vaccine microorganisms will somehow spring back to life, causing the diseases they were meant to forestall. For that reason, vaccine makers today favor so-called subunit preparations, composed primarily of antigenic proteins divorced from a pathogen's genes. On their own, the proteins have no way of establishing an infection. Subunit vaccines, however, are expensive, in part because they are produced in cultures of bacteria or animal cells and have to be purified out; they also need to be refrigerated.

Food vaccines are like subunit preparations in that they are engineered to contain antigens but bear no genes that would enable whole pathogens to form. Ten years ago Arntzen understood that edible vaccines would therefore be as safe as subunit preparations

How to Make an Edible Vaccine

One way of generating edible vaccines relies on the bacterium *Agrobacterium tumefaciens* to deliver into plant cells the genetic blueprints for viral or bacterial "antigens"—proteins that elicit a targeted immune response in the recipient. The diagram illustrates the production of vaccine potatoes.

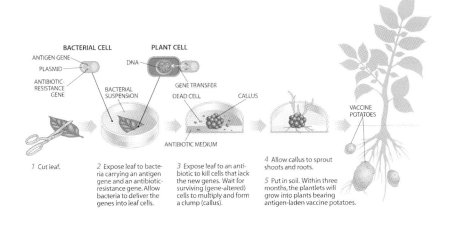

BACTERIAL CELL   PLANT CELL
ANTIGEN GENE
PLASMID
DNA
ANTIBIOTIC-
RESISTANCE
GENE
BACTERIAL
SUSPENSION
GENE TRANSFER
DEAD CELL   CALLUS
VACCINE
POTATOES
ANTIBIOTIC MEDIUM

1 Cut leaf.

2 Expose leaf to bacteria carrying an antigen gene and an antibiotic-resistance gene. Allow bacteria to deliver the genes into leaf cells.

3 Expose leaf to an antibiotic to kill cells that lack the new genes. Wait for surviving (gene-altered) cells to multiply and form a clump (callus).

4 Allow callus to sprout shoots and roots.

5 Put in soil. Within three months, the plantlets will grow into plants bearing antigen-laden vaccine potatoes.

while sidestepping their costs and demands for purification and refrigeration. But before he and others could study the effects of food vaccines in people, they had to obtain positive answers to a number of questions. Would plants engineered to carry antigen genes produce functional copies of the specified proteins? When the food plants were fed to test animals, would the antigens be degraded in the stomach before having a chance to act? (Typical subunit vaccines have to be delivered by injection precisely because of such degradation.) If the antigens did survive, would they, in fact, attract the immune system's attention? And would the response be strong enough to defend the animals against infection?

Additionally, researchers wanted to know whether edible vaccines would elicit what is known as mucosal immunity. Many pathogens enter the body through the nose, mouth or other openings. Hence, the first defenses they encounter are those in the mucous membranes that line the airways, the digestive tract and the reproductive tract; these membranes constitute the biggest pathogen-deterring surface in the body. When the mucosal immune response is effective, it generates molecules known as secretory antibodies that dash into the cavities of those passageways, neutralizing any pathogens they find. An effective reaction also activates a systemic response, in which circulating cells of the immune system help to destroy invaders at distant sites.

Injected vaccines initially bypass mucous membranes and typically do a poor job of stimulating mucosal immune responses. But edible vaccines come into contact with the lining of the digestive tract. In theory, then, they would activate both mucosal and systemic immunity. That dual effect should, in turn, help improve protection against many dangerous microorganisms, including, importantly, the kinds that cause diarrhea.

Those of us attempting to develop food vaccines place a high priority on combating diarrhea. Together the main causes—the Norwalk virus, rotavirus, *Vibrio cholerae* (the cause of cholera) and enterotoxigenic *Escherichia coli* (a toxin-producing source of "traveler's diarrhea")—account for some three million infant deaths a year, mainly in developing nations. These pathogens disrupt cells of the small intestine in ways that cause water to flow from the blood and tissues into the intestine. The resulting dehydration may be combated by delivering an intravenous or oral solution of electrolytes, but it often turns deadly when rehydration therapy is not an option. No vaccine practical for wide distribution in the developing nations is yet available to prevent these ills.

By 1995 researchers attempting to answer the many questions before them had established that plants could indeed manufacture foreign antigens in their proper conformations. For instance, Arntzen and his colleagues had introduced into tobacco plants the gene for a protein derived from the hepatitis B virus and had gotten the plants to synthesize the protein. When they injected the antigen into mice, it activated the same immune system components that are activated by the virus itself. (Hepatitis B can damage the liver and contribute to liver cancer.)

Green Lights on Many Fronts

But injection is not the aim; feeding is. In the past five years experiments conducted by Arntzen (who moved to the Boyce Thompson Institute for Plant Research at Cornell University in 1995) and his collaborators and by my group at Loma Linda University have demonstrated that tomato or potato plants can synthesize antigens from the Norwalk virus, enterotoxigenic *E. coli*, *V. cholerae* and the hepatitis B virus. Moreover, feeding antigen-laced tubers or fruits to test animals can evoke mucosal and systemic immune responses that fully or partly protect animals from subsequent exposure to the real pathogens or, in the case of *V. cholerae* and enterotoxigenic *E. coli*, to microbial toxins. Edible vaccines have also provided laboratory animals with some protection against challenge by the rabies virus, *Helicobacter pylori* (a bacterial cause of ulcers) and the mink enteric virus (which does not affect humans).

It is not entirely surprising that antigens delivered in plant foods survive the trip through the stomach well enough to reach and activate the immune system. The tough outer wall of plant cells apparently serves as temporary armor for the antigens, keeping them relatively safe from gastric secretions. When the wall finally begins to break up in the intestines, the cells gradually release their antigenic cargo.

Of course, the key question is whether food vaccines can be useful in people. The era of clinical trials for this technology is just beginning. Nevertheless, Arntzen and his collaborators obtained reassuring results in the first published human trial, involving about a dozen subjects. In 1997 volunteers who ate pieces of peeled, raw potatoes containing a benign segment of the *E. coli* toxin (the part called the B subunit) displayed both mucosal and systemic immune responses. Since then, the group has also seen immune reactivity in 19 of 20 people who ate a potato vaccine aimed at the Norwalk virus. Similarly, after Hilary Koprowski of Thomas Jefferson University fed transgenic lettuce carrying a hepatitis B antigen to three volunteers, two of the subjects displayed a good systemic response. Whether edible vaccines can actually protect against human disease remains to be determined, however.

Still to Be Accomplished

In short, the studies completed so far in animals and people have provided a proof of principle; they indicate that the strategy is feasible. Yet many issues must still be addressed. For one, the amount of vaccine made by a plant is low. Production can be increased in different ways—for instance, by linking antigen genes with regulatory elements known to help switch on the genes more readily. As researchers solve that challenge, they will also have to ensure that any given amount of a vaccine food provides a predictable dose of antigen.

Additionally, workers could try to enhance the odds that antigens will activate the immune system instead of passing out of the body unused. General stimulators (adjuvants) and better targeting to the immune system might compensate in part for low antigen production.

One targeting strategy involves linking antigens to molecules that bind well to immune system components known as M cells in the intestinal lining. M cells take in samples of materials that have entered the small intestine (including pathogens) and pass them to other cells of the immune system, such as antigen-presenting cells. Macrophages and other antigen-presenting cells chop up their acquisitions and display the resulting protein fragments on the cell surface. If white blood cells called helper T lymphocytes recognize the fragments as foreign, they may induce B lymphocytes (B cells) to secrete neutralizing antibodies and may also help initiate a broader attack on the perceived enemy.

It turns out that an innocuous segment of the *V. cholerae* toxin—the B subunit—binds readily to a molecule on M cells that ushers foreign material into those cells. By fusing antigens from other pathogens to this subunit, it should be possible to improve the uptake of antigens by M cells and to enhance immune responses to the added antigens. The B subunit also tends to associate with copies of itself, forming a doughnut-shaped, five-membered ring with a hole in the middle. These features raise the prospect of producing a vaccine that brings several different antigens to M cells at once—thus potentially fulfilling an urgent need for a single vaccine that can protect against multiple diseases simultaneously.

Researchers are also grappling with the reality that plants sometimes grow poorly when they start producing large amounts of a foreign protein. One solution would be to equip plants with regulatory elements that cause antigen genes to turn on—that is, give rise to the encoded antigens—only at selected times (such as after a plant is nearly fully grown or is exposed to some outside activator molecule) or only in its edible regions. This work is progressing.

Further, each type of plant poses its own challenges. Potatoes are ideal in many ways because they can be propagated from "eyes" and can be stored for long

How Edible Vaccines Provide Protection

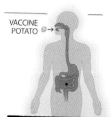

VACCINE POTATO

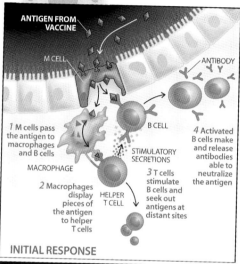

ANTIGEN FROM VACCINE

M CELL

ANTIBODY

B CELL

1 M cells pass the antigen to macrophages and B cells

MACROPHAGE

STIMULATORY SECRETIONS

4 Activated B cells make and release antibodies able to neutralize the antigen

3 T cells stimulate B cells and seek out antigens at distant sites

2 Macrophages display pieces of the antigen to helper T cells

HELPER T CELL

INITIAL RESPONSE

An antigen in a food vaccine gets taken up by M cells in the intestine (*left*) and passed to various immune-system cells, which then launch a defensive attack—as if the antigen were a true infectious agent, not just part of one. That response leaves long-lasting "memory" cells able to promptly neutralize the real infectious agent if it attempts an invasion (*below, left*).

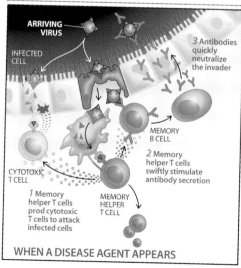

ARRIVING VIRUS

INFECTED CELL

3 Antibodies quickly neutralize the invader

MEMORY B CELL

2 Memory helper T cells swiftly stimulate antibody secretion

CYTOTOXIC T CELL

1 Memory helper T cells prod cytotoxic T cells to attack infected cells

MEMORY HELPER T CELL

WHEN A DISEASE AGENT APPEARS

periods without refrigeration. But potatoes usually have to be cooked to be palatable, and heating can denature proteins. Indeed, as is true of tobacco plants, potatoes were not initially intended to be used as vaccine vehicles; they were studied because they were easy to manipulate. Surprisingly, though, some kinds of potatoes are actually eaten raw in South America. Also, contrary to expectations, cooking of potatoes does not always destroy the full complement of antigen. So potatoes may have more practical merit than most of us expected.

Bananas need no cooking and are grown widely in developing nations, but banana trees take a few years to mature, and the fruit spoils fairly rapidly after ripening. Tomatoes grow more quickly and are cultivated broadly, but they too may rot readily. Inexpensive methods of preserving these foods—such as drying—might overcome the spoilage problem. Among the other foods under consideration are lettuce, carrots, peanuts, rice, wheat, corn and soybeans.

In another concern, scientists need to be sure that vaccines meant to enhance immune responses do not backfire and suppress immunity instead. Research into a phenomenon called oral tolerance has shown that ingesting certain proteins can at times cause the body to shut down its responses to those proteins. To determine safe, effective doses and feeding schedules for edible vaccines, manufacturers will need to gain a better handle on the manipulations that influence whether an orally delivered antigen will stimulate or depress immunity.

Moving Against Malnutrition

As research into edible vaccines is progressing, so too are efforts to make foods more nutritious. A much publicized example, "golden rice," takes aim at vitamin A deficiency, rampant in many parts of Asia, Africa and Latin America. This condition can lead to blindness and to immune impairment, which contributes to the death of more than a million children each year.

Rice would be a convenient way to deliver the needed vitamin, because the grain is a daily staple for a third or more of all people on the earth. But natural varieties do not supply vitamin A. Golden rice, though, has been genetically altered to make beta-carotene, a pigment the body converts to vitamin A.

A team led by Ingo Potrykus of the Swiss Federal Institute of Technology and Peter Beyer of the University of Freiburg in Germany formally reported its creation this past January in *Science*. In May an agribusiness—Zeneca—bought the rights and agreed to allow the rice to be donated to facilities that will cross the beta-carotene trait into rice species popular in impoverished areas and will distribute the resulting products to farmers at no charge. (Zeneca is hoping to make its money from sales of the improved rice in richer countries, where beta-carotene's antioxidant properties are likely to have appeal.)

Golden rice is not yet ready to be commercialized, however. Much testing still lies ahead, including analyses of whether the human body can efficiently absorb the beta-carotene in the rice. Testing is expected to last at least until 2003.

Meanwhile scientists are trying to enrich rice with still more beta-carotene, with other vitamins and with minerals. At a conference last year Potrykus announced success with iron; more than two billion people worldwide are iron deficient.

Investigators are attempting to enhance other foods as well. In June, for instance, a group of British and Japanese investigators reported the creation of a tomato containing a gene able to supply three times the usual amount of beta-carotene. Conventional breeding methods are being used, too, such as in an international project focused on increasing the vitamin and mineral content of rice and four other staples—wheat, corn, beans and cassava.

Not everyone is thrilled by the recent genetic coups. Genetically modified (GM) foods in general remain controversial. Some opponents contend that malnutrition can be combated right now in other ways—say, by constructing supply roads. And they fear that companies will tout the benefits of the new foods to deflect attention from worries over other GM crops, most of which (such as plants designed to resist damage from pesticides) offer fewer clear advantages for consumers. High on the list of concerns are risk to the environment and to people. Supporters of the nutritionally improved foods hope, however, that the rice won't be thrown out with the rinse water.

—*Ricki Rusting, staff writer*

A final issue worth studying is whether food vaccines ingested by mothers can indirectly vaccinate their babies. In theory, a mother could eat a banana or two and thus trigger production of antibodies that would travel to her fetus via the placenta or to her infant via breast milk.

Nonscientific challenges accompany the technical ones. Not many pharmaceutical manufacturers are eager to support research for products targeted primarily to markets outside the lucrative West. International aid organizations and some national governments and philanthropies are striving to fill the gap, but the effort to develop edible vaccines remains underfunded.

In addition, edible vaccines fall under the increasingly unpopular rubric of "genetically modified" plants. Recently a British company (Axis Genetics) that was supporting studies of edible vaccines failed; one of its leaders lays at least part of the blame on investor worry about companies involved with genetically engineered foods. I hope, however, that these vaccines will avoid serious controversy, because they are intended to save lives and would probably be planted over much less acreage than other food plants (if they are raised outside of greenhouses at all). Also, as drugs, they would be subjected to closer scrutiny by regulatory bodies.

Fighting Autoimmunity

Consideration of one of the challenges detailed here— the risk of inducing oral tolerance—has recently led my group and others to pursue edible vaccines as tools for quashing autoimmunity. Although oral delivery of antigens derived from infectious agents often stimulates the immune system, oral delivery of "autoantigens" (proteins derived from uninfected tissue in a treated individual) can sometimes suppress immune activity— a phenomenon seen frequently in test animals. No one fully understands the reasons for this difference.

Some of the evidence that ingesting autoantigens, or "self-antigens," might suppress autoimmunity comes from studies of type I diabetes, which results from autoimmune destruction of the insulin-producing cells (beta cells) of the pancreas. This destruction progresses silently for a time. Eventually, though, the loss of beta cells leads to a drastic shortage of insulin, a hormone needed to help cells take up sugar from the blood for energy. The loss results in high blood sugar levels. Insulin injections help to control diabetes, but they are by no means a cure; diabetics face an elevated risk of severe complications.

In the past 15 years, investigators have identified several beta cell proteins that can elicit autoimmunity in people predisposed to type I diabetes. The main culprits, however, are insulin and a protein called GAD (glutamic acid decarboxylase). Researchers have also made progress in detecting when diabetes is "brewing." The next step, then, is to find ways of stopping the underground process before any symptoms arise.

To that end, my colleagues and I, as well as other groups, have developed plant-based diabetes vaccines, such as potatoes containing insulin or GAD linked to

Stopping Autoimmunity

The autoimmune reaction responsible for type I diabetes arises when the immune system mistakes proteins that are made by pancreatic beta cells (the insulin producers) for foreign invaders. The resulting attack, targeted to the offending proteins, or "autoantigens," destroys the beta cells (*below, left*). Eating small amounts of autoantigens quiets the process in diabetic mice, for unclear reasons. The autoantigens might act in part by switching on "suppressor" cells of the immune system (*inset*), which then block the destructive activities of their cousins (*below, right*).

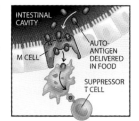

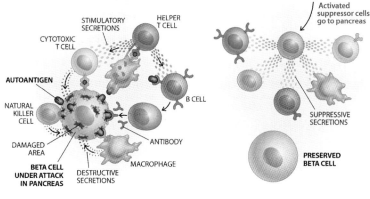

BEFORE TREATMENT

AFTER TREATMENT

the innocuous B subunit of the *V. cholerae* toxin (to enhance uptake of the antigens by M cells). Feeding of the vaccines to a mouse strain that becomes diabetic helped to suppress the immune attack and to prevent or delay the onset of high blood sugar.

Transgenic plants cannot yet produce the amounts of self-antigens that would be needed for a viable vaccine against human diabetes or other autoimmune diseases.

But, as is true for infectious diseases, investigators are exploring a number of promising schemes to overcome that and other challenges.

Edible vaccines for combating autoimmunity and infectious diseases have a long way to go before they will be ready for large-scale testing in people. The technical obstacles, though, all seem surmountable. Nothing would be more satisfying than to protect the health of many millions of now defenseless children around the globe.

Further Information

Oral Immunization with a Recombinant Bacterial Antigen Produced in Transgenic Plants. Charles J. Arntzen in *Science*, Vol. 268, No. 5211, pages 714–716; May 5, 1995.

Immunogenicity in Humans of a Recombinant Bacterial Antigen Delivered in a Transgenic Potato. C. O. Tacket et al. in *Nature Medicine*, Vol. 4, No. 5, pages 607–609; May 1998.

A Plant-Based Cholera Toxin B Subunit-Insulin Fusion Protein Protects against the Development of Autoimmune Diabetes. Takeshi Arakawa, Jie Yu, D. K. Chong, John Hough, Paul C. Engen and William H. R. Langridge in *Nature Biotechnology*, Vol. 16, No. 10, pages 934–938; October 1998.

Plant-Based Vaccines for Protection against Infectious and Autoimmune Diseases. James E. Carter and William H. R. Langridge in *Critical Reviews in Plant Sciences* (in press).

About the Author

WILLIAM H. R. LANGRIDGE, a leader in the effort to develop edible vaccines for infectious and autoimmune diseases, is professor in the department of biochemistry and at the Center for Molecular Biology and Gene Therapy at the Loma Linda University School of Medicine. After receiving his Ph.D. in biochemistry from the University of Massachusetts at Amherst in 1973, he conducted genetic research on insect viruses and plants at the Boyce Thompson Institute for Plant Research at Cornell University. In 1987 he moved to the Plant Biotechnology Center of the University of Alberta in Edmonton, and he joined Loma Linda in 1993.

"The Unmet Challenges
4. of Hepatitis C"

By Adrian M. Di Bisceglie and Bruce R. Bacon

Some 1.8 percent of the U.S. adult population are infected with the hepatitis C virus, most without knowing it.

As recently as the late 1980s few people other than physicians had heard of hepatitis C, a slowly progressing viral infection that over a couple of decades can lead to liver failure or liver cancer. Today the condition is widely recognized as a huge public health concern. Some 1.8 percent of the U.S. adult population, almost four million people, are infected with the hepatitis C virus, most of them without knowing it. The virus is one of the major causes of chronic liver disease, probably accounting for even more cases than excessive alcohol use, and is the most common reason for liver transplants. Some 9,000 people die each year in the U.S. from complications of the infection, a number that is expected to triple by 2010. Information about the incidence of hepatitis C in other countries is less reliable, but it is clear that the virus is a major public health problem throughout the world.

Physicians, historians and military leaders have long recognized hepatitis—inflammation of the liver—as a cause of jaundice. This yellow discoloration of the whites of the eyes and skin occurs when the liver fails to excrete a pigment called bilirubin, which then accumulates in the body. In recent decades, however, the diagnosis of hepatitis has progressively improved, and physicians can now distinguish several distinct forms. At least five different viruses can cause the condition, as can drugs and toxins such as alcohol.

Researchers first studied viral hepatitis in the 1930s and 1940s in settings where jaundice was common, such as prisons and mental institutions. They identified two distinct forms with different patterns of transmission. One was transmitted by contact with feces of infected individuals and was called infectious hepatitis, or hepatitis A. The other appeared to be passed only through blood and was termed serum hepatitis, or hepatitis B.

An important development occurred in the 1950s, when researchers devised tests for liver injury based on certain enzymes in blood serum. When liver cells—known as hepatocytes—die, they release these enzymes into the circulation, where their concentrations can be easily measured. Elevated serum levels of alanine aminotransferase (ALT) and, especially, aspartate aminotransferase (AST) became recognized as more reliable signs of liver trouble than jaundice. (In addition to hepatitis, some uncommon inherited metabolic diseases can cause elevated liver enzymes.)

There things stood until Baruch Blumberg, working at the National Institutes of Health, made a breakthrough in the mid-1960s. Blumberg identified the signature of a viral agent, now known as hepatitis B virus, in the blood of patients with that disease. Blumberg's discovery won him a Nobel Prize and allowed researchers to develop reliable blood tests for the virus. A decade later Stephen M. Feinstone, a researcher at the same institution, identified a different viral agent in the stool of patients with hepatitis A. This work led quickly to the development of tests that accurately detect antibodies to hepatitis A virus in the blood of those infected.

Hepatitis had long been a significant risk for recipients of blood transfusions and blood products. As many as 30 percent of patients receiving a blood transfusion in the 1960s developed elevated levels of ALT and AST, or even jaundice, some weeks later. Workers had suspected an infectious agent was responsible. When the new tests for hepatitis A and B became available in the 1970s, researchers soon found that a substantial proportion of cases of post-transfusion hepatitis were caused by neither of these two viruses. The new disease was labeled "non-A, non-B" hepatitis.

Most investigators expected that the agent responsible for these cases would soon be discovered. In reality, it took nearly 15 years before Michael Houghton and his colleagues at Chiron Corporation, a biotechnology company in Emeryville, Calif., finally identified the hepatitis C virus, using samples of serum from infected chimpanzees provided by Daniel W. Bradley of the Centers for Disease Control and Prevention. Hepatitis C accounts for most cases of viral hepatitis that are not types A or B, although a few result from other, rarer viruses.

The Needle in an RNA Haystack

Hepatitis C virus proved difficult to identify because it cannot be reliably grown in cell cultures, and chimpanzees and tamarins appear to be the only nonhuman animals that can be infected. Because both species are very expensive to use in research, only small numbers of animals can be employed. These obstacles, which still impede the study of the virus, explain why it was the first infectious agent discovered entirely by cloning nucleic acid.

The Chiron researchers first extracted RNA from serum samples strongly suspected to contain the unknown viral agent. A chemical variant of DNA, RNA is used by many viruses as their genetic material. RNA is also found in healthy cells, so the problem was to identify the tiny fraction corresponding to the unknown viral genome.

The Chiron workers used an enzyme to copy multiple fragments of DNA from the RNA, so that each carried some part of its genetic sequence. Next, they inserted this "complementary DNA" into viruslike entities that infect *Escherichia coli* bacteria, which induced some bacteria to manufacture protein fragments that the DNA encoded. The researchers grew the bacteria to form colonies, or clones, that were then tested for their ability to cause a visible reaction with serum from chimpanzees and a human with non-A, non-B hepatitis.

The hope was that antibodies in the serum would bind to any clones producing protein from the infectious agent. Out of a million bacterial clones tested, just one was found that reacted with serum from chimpanzees with the disease but not with serum from the same chimpanzees before they had been infected. The result indicated that this clone contained genetic sequences of the disease agent. Using the clone as a toehold, investigators subsequently characterized the remainder of the virus's genetic material and developed the first diagnostic assay, a test that detects antibodies to hepatitis C in blood. Since 1990 that test and subsequent versions have allowed authorities to screen all blood donated to blood banks for signs of infection.

The antibody test soon showed hepatitis C to be a much bigger threat to public health than had generally been recognized. A remarkable feature—one that sets it apart from most other viruses—is its propensity to cause chronic disease. Most other viruses are self-limited: infection with hepatitis A, for example, usually lasts for only a few weeks. In contrast, nearly 90 percent of people with hepatitis C have it for years or decades.

Few patients know the source of their virus, but on direct questioning many recall having a blood transfusion, an episode of injection drug use or an injury from a hypodermic needle containing blood from an infected individual. About 40 percent of patients have none of these clear risk factors but fall into one of several categories identified in epidemiologic studies.

These include having had sexual contact with someone with hepatitis, having had more than one sexual partner in the past year, and being of low socioeconomic status.

Whether hepatitis C is sexually transmitted is controversial. Instances of transmission between partners in stable, monogamous relationships are rarely identified, and the rate of infection in promiscuous gay men is no higher than in the population in general. These observations suggest that sexual transmission is uncommon, but they are hard to reconcile with the epidemiologic findings. The paradox has not been resolved. Some patients who deny injection drug use may be unwilling or unable to recall it. Others might have been infected from unsterile razors or tattooing instruments. Shared straws put into the nose and used to snort street drugs might also transmit the virus via minute amounts of blood.

Slow Progress

The discovery of hepatitis C virus and the development of an accurate test for it mark an important victory for public health. The formerly substantial risk of infection from a blood transfusion has been virtually eliminated. Moreover, the rate of infection appears to be dropping among injection drug users, although this may be because anti-AIDS campaigns have discouraged sharing of needles. Yet hepatitis C still presents numerous challenges, and the prospects for eradicating the virus altogether appear dismal. Attempts to develop a vaccine have been hampered because even animals that successfully clear the virus from their bodies acquire no immunity to subsequent infection. Moreover, millions of people who are chronically infected are at risk of developing severe liver disease.

The mechanism of damage is known in outline. Viral infections can cause injury either because the virus kills cells directly or because the immune system attacks infected cells. Hepatitis C virus causes disease through the second mechanism. The immune system has two operating divisions. The humoral arm, which is responsible for producing antibodies, appears to be largely ineffective against hepatitis C virus. Although it produces antibodies to various viral components, the antibodies fail to neutralize the invader, and their presence does not indicate immunity, as is the case with hepatitis B.

It seems likely that hepatitis C virus evades this defense through its high mutation rate, particularly in regions of its genome responsible for the manufacture of proteins on the outside of the virus to which antibodies might bind. Two such hypervariable regions have been identified within the so-called envelope regions of the genome. As many as six distinct genotypes and many more subtypes of the virus have been identified; numerous variants exist even within a single patient.

In contrast to the humoral arm, the cellular arm of the immune system, which specializes in viral infections, mounts a vigorous defense against hepatitis C. It appears to be responsible for most of the liver injury. Cytotoxic

T lymphocytes primed to recognize hepatitis C proteins are found in the circulation and in the liver of chronically infected individuals and are thought to kill hepatocytes that display viral proteins. Fortunately, liver tissue can regenerate well, but that from hepatitis patients often contains numerous dead or dying hepatocytes, as well as chronic inflammatory cells such as lymphocytes and monocytes.

Long-Term Consequences

If hepatitis persists for long enough—typically some years—the condition escalates, and normally quiescent cells adjacent to hepatocytes, called hepatic stellate cells, become abnormally activated. These cells then secrete collagen and other proteins, which disrupt the fine-scale structure of the liver and slowly impair its ability to process materials. This pathology is known as fibrosis. Stellate cells are similar in origin and function to the fibrosis-producing cells found in other organs, such as fibroblasts in the skin and mesangial cells in the kidney. They store vitamin A as well as produce the liver's extracellular matrix, or framework. It is likely that many of the processes that initiate the fibrotic response in the liver occur in these other tissues as well.

If fibrosis progresses far enough, it results in cirrhosis, which is characterized by bands of fibrosis enclosing nodules of regenerating hepatocytes. Progression is faster in people over age 50 at the time of infection, in those who consume more than 50 grams of alcohol a day, and in men, but cirrhosis can result even in patients who never drink alcohol. Fibrosis and cirrhosis are generally considered irreversible, although recent findings cast some doubt on that conclusion.

About 20 percent of patients develop cirrhosis over the first 20 years of infection. Thereafter some individuals may reach a state of equilibrium without further liver damage, whereas others may continue to experience very slow but progressive fibrosis. End-stage liver disease often manifests itself as jaundice, ascites (accumulation of fluid within the abdomen), bleeding from varicose veins within the esophagus, and confusion. Hepatitis C infection has also come to be recognized as a major indirect cause of primary liver cancer. The virus itself seems not to put people at increased risk, but cirrhosis induced by the virus does.

Cirrhosis is responsible for almost all the illness caused by the hepatitis C virus. Although a small proportion of patients recollect an episode of jaundice when they probably acquired their infection, chronic hepatitis C is often asymptomatic. When symptoms do occur, they are nonspecific: patients sometimes complain of vague feelings of fatigue, nausea or general unwellness. The insidious nature of the condition is probably another reason why hepatitis C remained undiscovered for as long as it did. The disease plays out over decades. An aspect confounding investigators is that not all infected individuals react in the same way. Some may carry the virus for decades without significant injury; others experience serious damage within only a few years.

Liver transplantation can save some end-stage patients, but the supply of human livers available for transplant is woefully inadequate. Researchers are therefore working intensively to develop treatments that will eradicate the virus in patients.

The first therapeutic agent shown to be effective was alpha interferon, a protein that occurs naturally in the body. Interferon appears to have a nonspecific antiviral action and may also enhance immune system activity. The drug is generally given by subcutaneous injection three times a week for 12 months. Only 15 to 20 percent of patients, however, exhibit a sustained response, as defined by the return of ALT and AST to normal levels and the absence of detectable hepatitis C RNA in serum for at least six months after stopping treatment. Why treatment fails in most patients is essentially unknown, although some viral genotypes seem to be more susceptible to interferon than others.

Last year the Food and Drug Administration approved another drug, ribavirin, to treat hepatitis C in conjunction with interferon. Ribavirin, which can be swallowed in pill form, inhibits many viruses. Interestingly, though, it appears to have no effect against the hepatitis C virus by itself and is thought somehow to enhance interferon's effects on the immune system. Interferon and ribavirin given together for six to 12 months can expunge the virus in about 40 percent of patients, and clinical workers are now studying how to maximize the benefits from these two agents. Long-acting forms of interferon that require administration only once a week are one focus of interest.

A new drug is now being tested in small numbers of patients. Vertex Pharmaceuticals in Cambridge, Mass., is investigating a compound that inhibits a human enzyme called ionosine mono-phosphate dehydrogenase. The hepatitis C virus relies on this enzyme to generate constituents of RNA. No results from these trials are yet available.

In the absence of medications capable of dependably eliminating the virus, the NIH recently embarked on a study to determine whether long-term administration of alpha interferon can slow liver damage in patients who fail to clear the virus. And we and other researchers are studying the simple expedient of taking a pint of blood from patients on a regular basis. This treatment reduces the amount of iron in the body, a manipulation that can reduce serum ALT and AST levels. Whether it slows liver damage is still uncertain.

Targeting the Virus

The best prospects for future treatment for hepatitis C appear to be agents targeted specifically against the virus, just as successful treatments for HIV target that agent. With that goal in mind, researchers have elucidated the structure of the hepatitis C virus in detail. Its genetic material, or genome, consists of a single strand of RNA.

How the Hepatitis C Virus Was Discovered

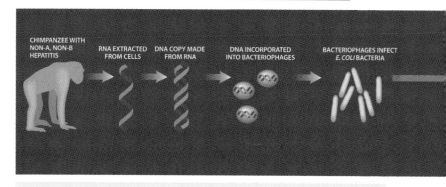

CHIMPANZEE WITH
NON-A, NON-B
HEPATITIS

RNA EXTRACTED
FROM CELLS

DNA COPY MADE
FROM RNA

DNA INCORPORATED
INTO BACTERIOPHAGES

BACTERIOPHAGES INFECT
E. COLI BACTERIA

Researchers identified the hepatitis C virus by making DNA copies of RNA from the cells of infected chimpanzees. They cloned the DNA by using bacteriophages to carry it into bacteria. Colonies were then tested with serum from infected chimps. One produced an immune reaction, indicating it carried viral genetic sequences.

—A.M.D. and B.R.B.

In size and organization the genome is similar to that of yellow fever and dengue fever viruses; hepatitis C virus has therefore been classified with them as a member of the family Flaviviridae. Enzymes in an infected cell use the viral RNA as a template to produce a single large protein called a polyprotein, which then cleaves to yield a variety of separate proteins with different functions. Some are structural proteins that go to form new viral particles; others are enzymes that replicate the original infecting RNA. At either end of the genome are short stretches of RNA that are not translated into protein. One of these terminal regions seems to prompt infected cells to manufacture the viral polyprotein; it is an

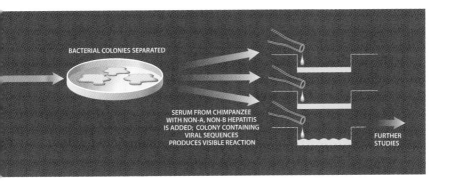

BACTERIAL COLONIES SEPARATED

SERUM FROM CHIMPANZEE WITH NON-A, NON-B HEPATITIS IS ADDED; COLONY CONTAINING VIRAL SEQUENCES PRODUCES VISIBLE REACTION

FURTHER STUDIES

important target for diagnostic assays. The other appears to play a role in initiating the replication of viral RNA.

The structural proteins include the core protein, which encloses the RNA in a viral particle within a structure known as the nucleocapsid, and two envelope proteins that coat the nucleocapsid. The nonstructural proteins include a viral protease responsible for cleaving the polyprotein, as well as other enzymes responsible for chemically readying the components of viral RNA (triphosphatase), for copying the RNA (polymerase) and for unwinding the newly manufactured copy (helicase).

The protease and helicase enzymes have been well characterized and their detailed three-dimensional structure elucidated through x-ray crystallography, necessary first steps for designing drugs to inhibit an enzyme. Several drug companies, including Schering-Plough, Agouron Pharmaceuticals, and Eli Lilly and Vertex Pharmaceuticals, are now studying potential hepatitis C protease or helicase inhibitors. Clinical

How the Hepatitis C Virus Reproduces Itself

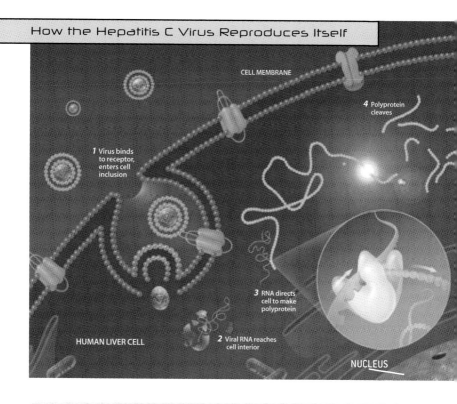

Hepatitis C infection starts when viral particles in the circulation find their way to susceptible cells, particularly hepatocytes. A viral protein called E2 appears to facilitate entry by latching onto a specific receptor. On entering, the virus loses its lipid coat and its protein envelope, freeing the RNA cargo. Enzymes in the cell then use this RNA as a template to make a large viral protein, the polyprotein. It is cleaved into a variety of small proteins that go on to form new viral particles and help to copy the viral RNA.

The original RNA is copied to yield a "negative-stranded" RNA that carries the inverse, or complement, of the original sequence. This serves as a template to make multiple copies of the original RNA, which are incorporated into new viral particles, along with structural proteins, at a body called the Golgi complex. Complete viral particles are eventually released from the infected cell, after acquiring a lipid surface layer. Recent studies suggest that a patient produces as many as 1,000 billion copies of hepatitis C virus a day, most of them from the liver.

—A.M.D. and B.R.B

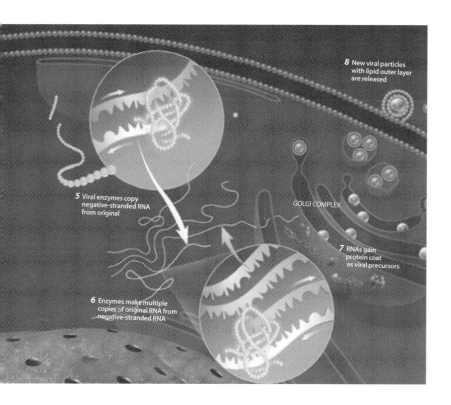

trials are probably only a few years away. Another viral enzyme, the polymerase, is also a possible target. Whether the virus will evolve resistance to such agents remains to be seen.

Developing anti–hepatitis C therapies may be about to get easier. Three months ago Ralf Bartenschlager and his colleagues at Johannes-Gutenberg University in Mainz, Germany, published details of an RNA genetic construct that includes the regions coding for the virus's enzymes and reproduces itself in liver cancer cell lines. This construct may prove valuable for testing drugs targeted at these enzymes.

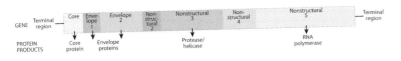

Hepatitis C virus genome consists of a single RNA gene plus two terminal regions. The gene encodes a polyprotein, which subsequently cleaves to form a variety of smaller proteins. Some of these are used to make new virus particles; others are enzymes that help to replicate the viral RNA for inclusion into new viruses.

Another possible therapeutic avenue being investigated is disruption of the process that activates hepatic stellate cells and causes them to instigate fibrosis. This mechanism is known to involve cytokines, or signaling chemicals, that cells in the liver called Kupffer cells release when they are stimulated by lymphocytes. Turning this process off once it has started should prevent most of the untoward consequences of hepatitis C infection.

Some workers are trying to develop therapeutics aimed at the short terminal regions of the virus's genome. One idea, being pursued by Ribozyme Pharmaceuticals, is to develop therapeutic molecules that can cut specific constant sequences there. Ribozymes, short lengths of RNA or a chemical close relative, can accomplish this feat. The main challenge may be getting enough ribozymes into infected cells. Delivering adequate quantities of a therapeutic agent is also a problem for some other innovative treatment concepts, such as gene therapy to make liver cells resistant to infection, "antisense" RNA that can inhibit specified genes, and engineered proteins that activate a cell's self-destruct mechanism when they are cleaved by the hepatitis C protease.

All these attempts to counter hepatitis C are hampered by a serious shortage of funds for research. The amount of federal support, considering the threat to millions of patients, is relatively small. We are confident that much improved therapies, and possibly a vaccine, will in time be available. An expanded research program could ensure that these developments come soon enough to help patients and those at risk.

Further Reading

The Crystal Structure of Hepatitis C Virus NS3 Proteinase Reveals a Trypsin-like Fold and a Structural Zinc Binding Site. Robert A. Love et al. in *Cell*, Vol. 87, No. 2, pages 331–342; October 18, 1996.

Management of Hepatitis C. National Institutes of Health Consensus Development Conference Panel Statement. In *Hepatology*, Vol. 26, Supplement No. 1, pages 2S–10S; 1997.

Interferon Alfa-2b Alone or in Combination with Ribavirin as Initial Treatment for Chronic Hepatitis C. John G. McHutchison et al. in *New England Journal of Medicine*, Vol. 339, No. 21, pages 1485–1492; November 19, 1998.

Molecular Characterization of Hepatitis C Virus. Second edition. Karen E. Reed and Charles M. Rice in *Hepatitis C Virus*. Edited by H. W. Reesink. Karger, Basel, 1998.

Replication of Subgenomic Hepatitis C Virus RNAs in a Hepatoma Cell Line. V. Lohmann, F. Körner, J.-O. Koch, U. Herian, L. Theilmann and R. Bartenschlager in *Science*, Vol. 285, pages 110–113; July 2, 1999.

About the Authors

ADRIAN M. DI BISCEGLIE and *BRUCE R. BACON* are physicians specializing in hepatitis C. Di Bisceglie received his medical training at the University of the Witwatersrand in South Africa. Before joining Saint Louis University School of Medicine as associate chairman of internal medicine, he was head of the liver diseases section at the National Institutes of Health. His research interests include viral hepatitis and primary liver cancer. Bacon is director of the division of gastroenterology and hepatology at Saint Louis University School of Medicine. He completed his medical training at Cleveland Metropolitan General Hospital. His research has focused on iron metabolism in the liver. Both Di Bisceglie and Bacon are associated with the American Liver Foundation: Di Bisceglie as medical director and Bacon as a member of the board of directors.

"Attacking
5. Anthrax"

By John A. T. Young and R. John Collier

Recent discoveries are suggesting much-needed strategies for improving prevention and treatment. High on the list: ways to neutralize the anthrax bacterium's fiendish toxin.

The need for new anthrax therapies became all too clear last fall when five people died of inhalation anthrax, victims of the first purposeful release of anthrax spores in the U.S. Within days of showing initially unalarming symptoms, the patients were gone, despite intensive treatment with antibiotics. Six others became seriously ill as well before pulling through.

Fortunately, our laboratories and others began studying the causative bacterium, *Bacillus anthracis*, and seeking antidotes long before fall 2001. Recent findings are now pointing the way to novel medicines and improved vaccines. Indeed, in the past year alone, the two of us and our collaborators have reported on three promising drug prototypes.

An Elusive Killer

The new ideas for fighting anthrax have emerged from ongoing research into how *B. anthracis* causes disease and death. Anthrax does not spread from individual to individual. A person (or animal) gets sick only after incredibly hardy spores enter the body through a cut in the skin, through contaminated food or through spore-laden air. Inside the body the spores molt into "vegetative," or actively dividing, cells.

Anthrax bacteria that colonize the skin or digestive tract initially do damage locally and may cause self-limited ailments: black sores and swelling in the first instance; possibly vomiting and abdominal pain and bleeding in the second. If bacterial growth persists unchecked in the skin or gastrointestinal tract, however, the microbes may eventually invade the bloodstream and thereby cause systemic disease.

Inhaled spores that reach deep into the lungs tend to waste little time where they land. They typically convert to the vegetative form and travel quickly to lymph nodes in the middle of the chest, where many of the cells find ready access to the blood. (Meanwhile bacteria that remain in the chest set the stage for a breath-robbing buildup of fluid around the lungs.)

Overview/Anthrax

- A three-part toxin produced by the anthrax bacterium, *Bacillus anthracis*, contributes profoundly to the symptoms and lethality of anthrax.
- The toxin causes trouble only when it gets into the cytosol of cells, the material that bathes the cell's internal compartments.
- Drugs that prevented the toxin from reaching the cytosol would probably go a long way toward limiting illness and saving the lives of people infected by the anthrax bacterium.
- Analyses of how the toxin enters cells have recently led to the discovery of several potential antitoxins.

Extensive replication in the blood is generally what kills patients who succumb to anthrax. *B. anthracis's* ability to expand so successfully derives from its secretion of two substances, known as virulence factors, that can profoundly derail the immune defenses meant to keep bacterial growth in check. One of these factors encases the vegetative cells in a polymer capsule that inhibits ingestion by the immune system's macrophages and neutrophils—the scavenger cells that normally degrade disease-causing bacteria. The capsule's partner in crime is an extraordinary toxin that works its way into those scavenger cells, or phagocytes, and interferes with their usual bacteria-killing actions.

The anthrax toxin, which also enters other cells, is thought to contribute to mortal illness not only by dampening immune responses but also by playing a direct role. Evidence for this view includes the observation that the toxin alone, in the absence of bacteria, can kill animals. Conversely, inducing the immune system to neutralize the toxin prevents *B. anthracis* from causing disease.

A Terrible Toxin

Harry Smith and his co-workers at the Microbiological Research Establishment in Wiltshire, England, discovered the toxin in the 1950s. Aware of its central part in anthrax's lethality, many researchers have since focused on learning how the substance "intoxicates" cells—gets into them and disrupts their activities. Such details offer essential clues to blocking its effects. Stephen H. Leppla and Arthur M. Friedlander, while at the U.S. Army Medical Research Institute of Infectious Diseases, initiated that effort with their colleagues in the 1980s; the two of us and others took up the task somewhat later.

The toxin turns out to consist of three proteins: protective antigen, edema factor and lethal factor. These proteins cooperate but are not always joined together physically. They are harmless individually until they attach to and enter cells, which they accomplish in a highly orchestrated fashion.

First, protective antigen binds to the surface of a cell, where an enzyme trims off its outermost tip. Next, seven of those trimmed molecules combine to form a ring-shaped structure, or heptamer, that captures the two factors and is transported to an internal membrane-bound compartment called an endosome. Mild acidity in this compartment causes the heptamer to change shape in a way that leads to the transport of edema factor and lethal factor across the endosomal membrane into the cytosol (the internal matrix of cells), where they do their mischief. In essence, the heptamer is like a syringe loaded with edema factor and lethal factor, and the slight acidity of the endosome causes the syringe to pierce the membrane of the endosome and inject the toxic factors into the cytosol.

Edema factor and lethal factor catalyze different molecular reactions in cells. Edema factor upsets the controls on ion and water flow across cell membranes

and thereby promotes the swelling of tissues. In phagocytes, it also saps energy that would otherwise be used
to engulf bacteria.

The precise behavior of lethal factor, which could be
more important in causing patient deaths, is less clear.
Scientists do know that it is a protease (a protein-
cutting enzyme) and that it cleaves enzymes in a family
known as MAPKKs. Now they are trying to tease out
the molecular events that follow such cleavage and to
uncover the factor's specific contributions to disease
and death.

Therapeutic Tactics

Certainly drugs able to neutralize the anthrax toxin
would help the immune system fight bacterial multipli-
cation and would probably reduce a patient's risk of
dying. At the moment, antibiotics given to victims of
inhalation anthrax may control microbial expansion
but leave the toxin free to wreak havoc.

In principle, toxin activity could be halted by interfering with any of the steps in the intoxication process.
An attractive approach would stop the sequence almost
before it starts, by preventing protective antigen from
attaching to cells. Scientists realized almost 10 years
ago that this protein initiated toxin entry by binding to
some specific protein on the surface of cells; when cells
were treated with enzymes that removed all their surface
proteins, protective antigen found no footing. Until very

recently, though, no one knew which of the countless proteins on cells served as the crucial receptor.

The two of us, with our colleagues Kenneth Bradley, Jeremy Mogridge and Michael Mourez, found the receptor last summer. Detailed analysis of this molecule (now named ATR, for anthrax toxin receptor) then revealed that it spans the cell membrane and protrudes from it. The protruding part contains an area resembling a region that serves in other receptors as an attachment site for particular proteins. This discovery suggested that the area was the place where protective antigen latched onto ATR, and indeed it is.

We have not yet learned the normal function of the receptor, which surely did not evolve specifically to allow the anthrax toxin into cells. Nevertheless, knowledge of the molecule's makeup is enabling us to begin testing inhibitors of its activity. We have had success, for instance, with a compound called sATR, which is a soluble form of the receptor domain that binds to protective antigen. When sATR molecules are mixed into the medium surrounding cells, they serve as effective decoys, tricking protective antigen into binding to them instead of to its true receptor on cells.

We are now trying to produce sATR in the amounts needed for evaluating its ability to combat anthrax in rodents and nonhuman primates—experiments that must be done before any new drug can be considered for fighting anthrax in people. Other groups are examining whether carefully engineered antibodies (highly specific molecules of the immune system) might bind tightly to protective antigen in ways that will keep it from coupling with its receptor.

More Targets

Scientists are also seeking ways to forestall later steps in the intoxication pathway. For example, a team from Harvard has constructed a drug able to clog the regions of the heptamer that grasp edema and lethal factors. The group—from the laboratories of one of us (Collier) and George M. Whitesides—reasoned that a plugged heptamer would be unable to draw the factors into cells.

We began by screening randomly constructed peptides (short chains of amino acids) to see if any of them bound to the heptamer. One did, so we examined its ability to block toxin activity. It worked, but weakly. Assuming that fitting many plugs into the heptamer's binding domains for edema and lethal factor would be more effective, we took advantage of chemical procedures devised by Whitesides's group and linked an average of 22 copies of the peptide to a flexible polymer. That construction showed itself to be a strong inhibitor of toxin action—more than 7,000 times better than the free peptide—both in cell cultures and in rats.

Another exciting agent, and the one probably closest to human testing, would alter the heptamer itself. This compound was discovered after Bret R. Sellman in Collier's group noted that when certain mutant forms of protective antigen were mixed with normal forms, the heptamers formed on cells as usual but were unable

Detecting Anthrax: Rapid Sensing Would Save Lives

By Rocco Casagrande

If a terrorist group spread anthrax spores into the open air, the release could affect large numbers of people but would probably go unnoticed until victims showed up at hospitals. Many would undoubtedly seek help too late to be saved by current therapies. Much illness could be prevented, however, if future defenses against anthrax attacks included sensors that raised an alarm soon after spores appeared in the environment. The needed instruments are not yet ready for deployment, but various designs that incorporate cutting-edge technology are being developed.

Environmental sensors must discriminate between disease-causing agents (pathogens) and the thousands of similar but harmless microorganisms that colonize air, water and soil. Most of the tools being investigated work by detecting unique molecules on the surface of the pathogens of interest or by picking out stretches of DNA found only in those organisms.

The Canary, which is being developed at the Massachusetts Institute of Technology Lincoln Laboratory, is an innovative example of the devices that detect pathogens based on unique surface molecules. The sensors of the Canary consist of living cells—B cells of the immune system—that have been genetically altered to emit light when their calcium levels change. Protruding from these cells are receptors that will bind only to a unique part of a surface molecule on a particular pathogen. When the cells in the sensor bind to their target, that binding triggers the release of calcium ions from stores within the cells, which in turn causes the cells to give off light. The Canary can discern more than one type of pathogen by running a sample through several cell-filled modules, each of which reacts to a selected microorganism.

The GeneXpert system, developed by Cepheid, in Sunnyvale, Calif., is an example of a gene-centered approach. It begins its work by extracting DNA from microorganisms in a sample. Then, if a pathogen of concern is present, small primers (strips of genetic material able to recognize specific short sequences of DNA) latch onto the ends of DNA fragments unique to the pathogen. Next, through a procedure called the polymerase chain reaction (PCR), the system makes many copies of the bound DNA, adding fluorescent labels to the new copies along the way. Within about 30 minutes GeneXpert can make enough DNA to reveal whether even a small amount of the worrisome organism inhabited the original sample.

This system contains multiple PCR reaction chambers with distinct primer sets to allow the detection of different pathogens simultaneously. Furthermore, the GeneXpert system could be used to determine whether the anthrax bacterium is present in a nasal swab taken from a patient in as little as half an hour, significantly faster than the time it takes for conventional microbiological techniques to yield results.

Instruments designed specifically to detect spores of the anthrax bacterium or of closely related microbes (such as the one that causes botulism) can exploit the fact that such spores are packed full of dipicolinic acid (DPA)—a compound, rarely found elsewhere in nature, that helps them to survive harsh environmental conditions. Molecules that fluoresce when bound to DPA have shown promise in chemically based anthrax detectors. "Electronic noses," such as the Cyranose detection system made by Cyrano Sciences in Pasadena, Calif., could possibly "smell" the presence of DPA in an air sample laced with anthrax spores.

The true danger of an anthrax release lies in its secrecy. If an attack is discovered soon after it occurs and if exposed individuals receive treatment promptly, victims have an excellent chance of surviving. By enhancing early detection, sensors based on the systems discussed above or on entirely different technologies could effectively remove a horrible weapon from a terrorist's arsenal.

Rocco Casagrande is a scientist at Surface Logix in Brighton, Mass., where he is developing methods and devices for detecting biological weapons.

to inject edema and lethal factors into the cytosol. Remarkably, some of these mutants were so disruptive that a single copy in a heptamer completely prevented injection.

In a study reported last April, these mutants—known as dominant negative inhibitors, or DNIs—proved to be potent blockers of the anthrax toxin in cell cultures and in rats. Relatively small amounts of selected DNIs neutralized an amount of protective antigen and lethal factor that would otherwise kill a rat in 90 minutes. These findings suggest that each mutant copy of protective antigen is capable of inactivating six normal copies in the bloodstream and that it would probably reduce toxin activity in patients dramatically.

Of course, as more and more questions about the toxin are answered, scientists should discover further treatment ideas. Now that the receptor for protective antigen has been identified, researchers can use it as a target in screening tests aimed at finding drugs able to bar the receptor from binding to protective antigen. And understanding of the receptor's three-dimensional structure would reveal the precise contact points between protective antigen and the receptor, enabling drugmakers to custom-design receptor blocking agents.

Scientists would also like to uncover the molecular interactions that enable protective antigen heptamers to move from the cell surface into endosomes inside the cell. Impeding that migration should be very useful. And what happens after lethal factor cleaves MAPKK enzymes? How do those subsequent events affect cells? Although the latter question remains a vexing challenge, recent study of lethal factor has brightened the prospects for finding drugs able to inactivate it. Last November, Robert C. Liddington of the Burnham Institute in La Jolla, Calif., and his colleagues in several laboratories published the three-dimensional structure of the part of lethal factor that acts on MAPKK molecules. That site can now become a target for drug screening or design.

New leads for drugs should also emerge from the recent sequencing of the code letters composing the *B. anthracis* genome. By finding genes that resemble those of known functions in other organisms, biologists are likely to discover additional information about how the anthrax bacterium causes disease and how to stop it.

The continuing research should yield several anti-toxins. To be most effective, such drugs will probably be used with antibiotics, much as cocktails of antiviral drugs are recommended for treating HIV infection.

Promising Preventives

As plans to improve therapies proceed, so does work on better vaccines. Vaccines against toxin-producing bacteria often prime the immune system to neutralize the toxin of concern as soon as it appears in the body, thus preventing disease. Livestock in parts of the U.S. receive preparations consisting of *B. anthracis* cells that lack the protective capsule and thus replicate poorly. A similar vaccine for humans has been used in the former Soviet Union. But preparations that contain whole microbes often cause side effects, and they raise the specter that renegade cells might at times give rise to the very diseases they were meant to prevent.

The only anthrax vaccine approved for human use in the U.S. takes a different form. It consists primarily of toxin molecules that have been chemically treated to prevent them from making people ill. It is produced by growing the weakened strain of *B. anthracis* in culture, filtering the bacterial cells from the culture medium, adsorbing the toxin proteins in the remaining filtrate onto an adjuvant (a substance that enhances immune responses) and treating the mixture with formaldehyde to inactivate the proteins. Injection of this preparation, known as AVA (for anthrax vaccine adsorbed), stimulates the immune system to produce antibodies that specifically bind to and inactivate the toxin's components. Most of

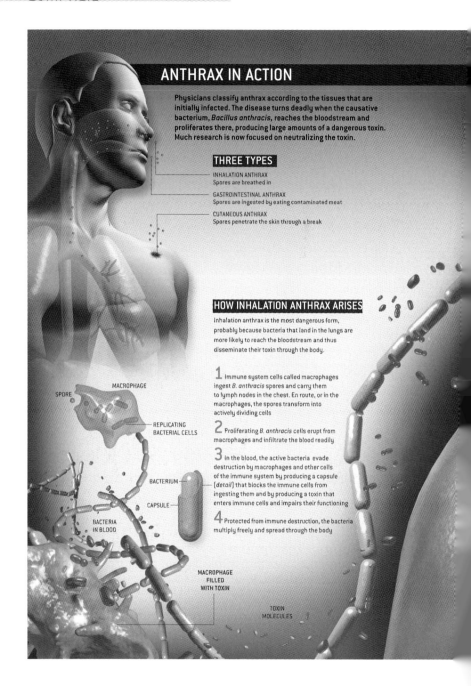

ANTHRAX IN ACTION

Physicians classify anthrax according to the tissues that are initially infected. The disease turns deadly when the causative bacterium, *Bacillus anthracis*, reaches the bloodstream and proliferates there, producing large amounts of a dangerous toxin. Much research is now focused on neutralizing the toxin.

THREE TYPES

INHALATION ANTHRAX
Spores are breathed in

GASTROINTESTINAL ANTHRAX
Spores are ingested by eating contaminated meat

CUTANEOUS ANTHRAX
Spores penetrate the skin through a break

HOW INHALATION ANTHRAX ARISES

Inhalation anthrax is the most dangerous form, probably because bacteria that land in the lungs are more likely to reach the bloodstream and thus disseminate their toxin through the body.

1 Immune system cells called macrophages ingest *B. anthracis* spores and carry them to lymph nodes in the chest. En route, or in the macrophages, the spores transform into actively dividing cells

2 Proliferating *B. anthracis* cells erupt from macrophages and infiltrate the blood readily

3 In the blood, the active bacteria evade destruction by macrophages and other cells of the immune system by producing a capsule (*detail*) that blocks the immune cells from ingesting them and by producing a toxin that enters immune cells and impairs their functioning

4 Protected from immune destruction, the bacteria multiply freely and spread through the body

MACROPHAGE

SPORE

REPLICATING
BACTERIAL CELLS

BACTERIUM

CAPSULE

BACTERIA
IN BLOOD

MACROPHAGE
FILLED
WITH TOXIN

TOXIN
MOLECULES

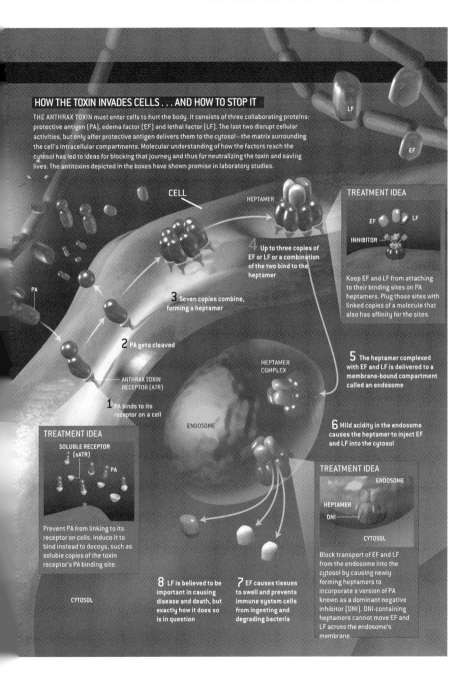

HOW THE TOXIN INVADES CELLS . . . AND HOW TO STOP IT

THE ANTHRAX TOXIN must enter cells to hurt the body. It consists of three collaborating proteins: protective antigen (PA), edema factor (EF) and lethal factor (LF). The last two disrupt cellular activities, but only after protective antigen delivers them to the cytosol—the matrix surrounding the cell's intracellular compartments. Molecular understanding of how the factors reach the cytosol has led to ideas for blocking that journey and thus for neutralizing the toxin and saving lives. The antitoxins depicted in the boxes have shown promise in laboratory studies.

LF

EF

CELL

HEPTAMER

TREATMENT IDEA

EF   LF

INHIBITOR

Keep EF and LF from attaching to their binding sites on PA heptamers. Plug those sites with linked copies of a molecule that also has affinity for the sites.

4 Up to three copies of EF or LF or a combination of the two bind to the heptamer

3 Seven copies combine, forming a heptamer

PA

2 PA gets cleaved

HEPTAMER COMPLEX

5 The heptamer complexed with EF and LF is delivered to a membrane-bound compartment called an endosome

ANTHRAX TOXIN RECEPTOR (ATR)

1 PA binds to its receptor on a cell

ENDOSOME

6 Mild acidity in the endosome causes the heptamer to inject EF and LF into the cytosol

TREATMENT IDEA

SOLUBLE RECEPTOR (sATR)

PA

Prevent PA from linking to its receptor on cells; induce it to bind instead to decoys, such as soluble copies of the toxin receptor's PA binding site.

CYTOSOL

TREATMENT IDEA

ENDOSOME

HEPTAMER

DNI

CYTOSOL

Block transport of EF and LF from the endosome into the cytosol by causing newly forming heptamers to incorporate a version of PA known as a dominant negative inhibitor (DNI). DNI-containing heptamers cannot move EF and LF across the endosome's membrane.

8 LF is believed to be important in causing disease and death, but exactly how it does so is in question

7 EF causes tissues to swell and prevents immune system cells from ingesting and degrading bacteria

the antibodies act on protective antigen, however, which explains the protein's name: it is the component that best elicits protective immunity.

AVA is given to soldiers and certain civilians but is problematic as a tool for shielding the general public against biological warfare. Supplies are limited. And even if AVA were available in abundance, it would be cumbersome to deliver on a large scale; the standard protocol calls for six shots delivered over 18 months followed by annual boosters. The vaccine has not been licensed for use in people already exposed to anthrax spores. But late last year officials, worried that spores might sometimes survive in the lungs for a long time, began offering an abbreviated, three-course dose on an experimental basis to postal workers and others who had already taken 60 days of precautionary antibiotics. People who accepted the offer were obliged to take antibiotics for an additional 40 days, after which the immunity stimulated by the vaccine would presumably be strong enough to provide adequate protection on its own.

In hopes of producing a more powerful, less cumbersome and faster-acting vaccine, many investigators are focusing on developing inoculants composed primarily of protective antigen produced by recombinant DNA technology. By coupling the recombinant protein with a potent new-generation adjuvant, scientists may be able to evoke good protective immunity relatively quickly with only one or two injections. The dominant negative inhibitors discussed earlier as possible treatments could be useful forms of protective antigen to choose. Those

Medical Lessons:
Doctors Now Have a Changed View of Inhalation Anthrax

By Ricki L. Rusting

The recent cases of inhalation anthrax in the U.S. have upended some old assumptions about that disease. When contaminated letters started appearing in September 2001, public health authorities initially believed that only those who received the letters, and perhaps individuals nearby, were in danger. But spores clearly seeped out through the weave of the envelopes, contaminating postal facilities and jumping to other mail. Such "cross contamination" is a leading explanation for the deaths of two of the 11 people confirmed to have contracted inhalation anthrax last year. Also contrary to expectations, spores do not remain sedentary once they land. They can become airborne again as people walk around in a tainted room.

One surprise was positive. Before October 2001 common wisdom held that inhalation anthrax was almost always incurable after symptoms appeared. But doctors beat those odds last fall, saving six of the victims. What made the difference? Researchers cannot draw firm conclusions from so few cases. But some intriguing patterns emerged when John A. Jernigan of the Centers for Disease Control and Prevention (CDC) and a team of others reviewed the medical records of the first 10 patients. Their findings appear in the November/December 2001 Emerging Infectious Diseases and online at www.cdc.gov/ncidod/eid/vol7no6/jernigan.htm

Relatively prompt diagnosis may have helped, the researchers report. Inhalation anthrax has two symptomatic phases—an early period marked by maladies common to a variety of ailments (such as fatigue, fever, aches and cough) and a later phase in which patients become critically ill with high fever, labored breathing and shock. Six of the 10 patients received antibiotics active against the anthrax bacterium, Bacillus anthracis, while they were still showing early symptoms of infection, and only they survived.

The types of antibiotics prescribed and the use of combinations of drugs might also have had a hand in the unexpectedly high survival rate. Nine of the people discussed in the review sought care before the CDC published what it called "interim" guidelines for treating inhalation anthrax on October 26, but most patients received therapy consistent with those guidelines: ciprofloxacin (the now famous Cipro) or doxycycline plus one or two other agents known to inhibit replication of B. anthracis (such as rifampin, vancomycin, penicillin, ampicillin, chloramphenicol, imipenem, clindamycin and clarithromycin). Aggressive "supportive" care—including draining dangerous fluid from around the lungs—probably helped as well, scientists say.

Even the survivors were very sick, however. Jernigan says they are still being observed to see whether long-term complications will develop, although as of mid-January no obvious signs of such problems had emerged. Researchers suspect that anthrax antitoxins would ease the course of many people afflicted with anthrax and might also rescue patients who could not be saved with current therapies.

Ricki L. Rusting is a staff editor and writer.

molecules retain their ability to elicit immune responses. Hence, they could do double duty: disarming the anthrax toxin in the short run while building up immunity that will persist later on.

We have no doubt that the expanding research on the biology of *B. anthracis* and on possible therapies and vaccines will one day provide a range of effective anthrax treatments. We fervently hope that these efforts will mean that nobody will have to die from anthrax acquired either naturally or as a result of biological terrorism.

More to Explore

Anthrax as a Biological Weapon: Medical and Public Health Management. Thomas V. Inglesby et al. in *Journal of the American Medical Association*, Vol. 281, No. 18, pages 1735–1745; May 12, 1999.

Dominant-Negative Mutants of a Toxin Subunit: An Approach to Therapy of Anthrax. Bret R. Sellman, Michael Mourez and R. John Collier in *Science*, Vol. 292, pages 695–697; April 27, 2001.

Designing a Polyvalent Inhibitor of Anthrax Toxin. Michael Mourez et al. in *Nature Biotechnology*, Vol. 19, pages 958–961; October 2001.

Identification of the Cellular Receptor for Anthrax Toxin. Kenneth A. Bradley, Jeremy Mogridge, Michael Mourez, R. John Collier and John A. T. Young in *Nature*, Vol. 414, pages 225–229; November 8, 2001.

The U.S. Centers for Disease Control and Prevention maintain a Web site devoted to anthrax at **www. cdc.gov/ncidod/dbmd/diseaseinfo/anthrax_g.htm.**

About the Authors

JOHN A. T. YOUNG and *R. JOHN COLLIER* have collaborated for several years on investigating the anthrax toxin. Young is Howard M. Temin Professor of Cancer Research in the McArdle Laboratory for Cancer Research at the University of Wisconsin–Madison. Collier, who has studied anthrax for more than 14 years, is Maude and Lillian Presley Professor of Microbiology and Molecular Genetics at Harvard Medical School.

"Shoot
6. This Deer"

By Philip Yam

Chronic wasting disease, a cousin of mad cow disease, is spreading among wild deer in parts of the U.S. Left unchecked, the fatal sickness could threaten North American deer populations—and maybe livestock and humans.

A place called the eradication zone, lying about 40 miles west of Madison, Wis., covers some 411 square miles. There thousands of white-tailed deer live—or rather, used to live.

Last year the Wisconsin Department of Natural Resources instituted special hunting periods to try to wipe out upward of 18,000 deer. During the fall, dead deer were taken to registration areas, where state employees in protective suits and gloves dragged carcasses from pickup trucks and lifted them onto plastic-covered picnic tables. With hacksaws, they severed the heads, double-bagged them and sent them for testing; the bodies themselves were incinerated.

The Dairy State's massacre is an attempt to keep a fatal ailment known as chronic wasting disease (CWD) from infecting its other 1.6 million deer. The testing enables wildlife officials to ascertain the scope of the epidemic—running at nearly 1.6 percent—and determine whether the culling can slow the spread. Currently no practical live test exists to check whether an apparently healthy, wild animal is actually incubating the sickness; only a brain sample will do.

The disease occurs because a pathogen peppers neural tissue full of microscopic holes and gums up the brain with toxic clumps of protein called amyloid plaques. Long confined to a patch of land near the Rocky Mountains, the disease has shown up in 12 states and two Canadian provinces. The sickness passes readily from one deer to another—no deer seem to have a natural resistance. "From everything we've seen," comments Michael W. Miller, a CWD expert with the Colorado Division of Wildlife, "it would persist. It would not go away on its own."

The urgency also reflects concern about the nature of CWD, which belongs to the same family as a better-known scourge: bovine spongiform encephalopathy (BSE), or mad cow disease. Spread by animal-based feed inadvertently containing tissue from sick cows and sheep, BSE emerged in the U.K. in the 1980s and continues to plague that country at a low level. (Nearly two dozen other countries have now also reported cases.) In 1996 scientists realized that BSE can pass to humans who eat infected meat, leading to a fatal condition: variant Creutzfeldt-Jakob disease, or vCJD (distinct from the more common sporadic CJD, which arises spontaneously in one in a million people). Researchers are now trying to figure out whether CWD could infect humans and livestock and thereby create an American version of the U.K.'s mad cow disaster.

Pathological Protein

The disease agent common to all these maladies is the prion ("PREE-on"), a term coined in 1982 by Stanley B. Prusiner of the University of California at San Francisco. The prion is a protein that exists in all animals, although the exact amino acid sequence depends on the species. It takes one of two shapes. Folded correctly, it is the normal prion protein (PrP), which is especially abundant in brain cells and may help process copper. Folded incorrectly, the prion protein becomes a pathogenic entity that kills. The malformed protein has the ability to refold copies of normal PrP in its own image, thereby making more of itself.

Prusiner's conception of prions initially met with great skepticism. That a pathogen could replicate and pass on its traits without assistance from nucleic acids (DNA or RNA) violated the orthodoxy of molecular biology. But enough evidence has accumulated to prove that some proteins can in fact copy themselves and that variants of PrP are essential players in spongiform encephalopathies.

That prions lack any DNA or RNA is also the prime reason why they are so tough. Germicidal light, formaldehyde baths and boiling water all promptly disrupt bacterial and viral nucleic acids, yet such treatments have little effect on malformed prions. Researchers have exposed prion-contaminated tissue to a dry heat of 600 degrees Celsius and left it buried for three years, only to find that the material, though greatly weakened, was still infectious. Indeed, physicians have unwittingly passed prion diseases on to patients via surgical instruments and transplanted organs that had undergone standard sterilization procedures. (Prion disinfection requires extended heating or corrosive chemicals such as sodium hydroxide.)

Foothold in the Foothills

The resilience of misfolded prions appears to be a key reason why chronic wasting disease has persisted and spread from its presumed starting point near Fort Collins, Colo. There, in 1967, at the state's Foothills Wildlife Research Facility, CWD made its first recorded appearance, in captive mule deer that were being maintained for nutritional studies (mule deer are the most common type in the West). As the name of the disease suggests, affected deer lose weight over the course of weeks or months. They often become thirsty, which drives them to drink large amounts of water

Overview/Chronic Wasting Disease

- Chronic wasting disease (CWD) is a fatal condition spreading among wild deer in some parts of North America. It kills in part by making holes in the brain.
- Malformed proteins called prions trigger the disease. The extreme durability of prions and CWD's long incubation times make controlling the spread of the sickness difficult.
- Studies are under way to see whether CWD can infect humans and livestock.

and, consequently, to urinate a great deal; they also start slobbering and drooling. They may stop socializing with fellow deer, become listless or hang their heads. Death typically ensues three to four months after symptoms start, although some victims expire within days and others in about a year. The incubation period, during which the animals show no symptoms, ranges from about 20 to 30 months.

The Fort Collins facility became a CWD death trap. Between 1970 and 1981, 90 percent of the deer that stayed more than two years died from the disease or had to be euthanized. In 1980 the scourge emerged outside Colorado, at the Sybille Research Unit in southeastern Wyoming, 120 miles northwest of Fort Collins. The two facilities had exchanged deer for breeding purposes, thus indicating that the disease was infectious—even to a different species: soon the elk at the facilities contracted the disease. (Deer and elk both belong to the cervid family.)

For years, researchers thought CWD resulted from nutritional deficiencies, poisoning, or stress from confinement. But in 1977 Elizabeth S. Williams, studying for her doctorate at Colorado State University, discovered that this view was mistaken. When Williams looked at brain slices from infected animals, she saw that the tissue was full of microscopic holes. "I happened to be taking a course in neuropathology and had studied a lot of brain lesions," she recalls. The holes were unmistakably like scrapie, the sheep sickness that was the first documented spongiform encephalopathy.

In fact, CWD appears to have originated from scrapie. Richard E. Race of the National Institutes of Health Rocky Mountain Laboratories in Hamilton, Mont., conducted test tube studies that revealed no distinction between the malformed PrP of scrapie sheep and CWD cervids. Consistent with this discovery, Amir Hamir of the U.S. Department of Agriculture's National Animal Disease Center in Ames, Iowa, found no difference in the appearance of brain samples from elk with CWD and elk experimentally infected with scrapie. (BSE also probably arose from scrapie, after cows ate feed derived from infected sheep.)

But unlike BSE in cows (or vCJD in humans), the cervids were not getting ill from their food. CWD behaves more like scrapie, in that the sickness spreads among individuals, although no one really knows how it does. The prions could lurk in the urine. During rutting season, deer bucks lap up the urine of perhaps dozens of does to find out which are in heat. Elk females lick males that have sprayed themselves with urine. Saliva could be a vector, too; in both deer and elk, individuals meet and greet by licking each other's mouths and noses, thus exchanging drool. Ranched elk may swap saliva when they feed in close quarters. It is also possible that animals take in the pathogen while grazing in areas where sick animals have shed prions on the ground in their feces, urine and saliva.

By 1985 veterinarians discovered CWD in free-ranging deer and elk, generally within about 30 miles of the two wildlife facilities. Whether the disease originated in the wild and spread to the captives, or vice versa, is not known. The two populations had plenty of time to mingle. Especially during mating season, wild cervids nosed up to captives through the chain-link fences. Incubating deer could also have escaped or been released.

Both facilities tried hard to eradicate CWD. The Sybille center killed all the deer and elk in the affected area and waited a year to introduce new animals; four years later deer and elk started coming down with CWD. The Fort Collins facility acted more aggressively. Officials first killed off all the resident deer and elk; then they turned several inches of soil and repeatedly sprayed structures and pastures with swimming-pool chlorine, which readily wipes out bacteria and viruses. After waiting a year, they brought in 12 elk calves, but a few years afterward two of those elk contracted CWD.

The disease's persistence has permanently contaminated an area of about 15,000 square miles in northeastern Colorado, southeastern Wyoming and (beginning in 2001) southwestern Nebraska. The incidence of CWD among the cervids in this so-called endemic area averages about 4 to 5 percent but has reached 18 percent in some places. To help keep the disease confined here, the research facilities stopped trading captive animals with each other. In fact, no captive cervids now leave the endemic area alive: "They're only allowed out to come to my necropsy room," wryly remarks Williams, now at the University of Wyoming. More important were the mountains and other natural barriers, which scientists expected would keep CWD from spreading rapidly out of the endemic area. There was, however, an easy way past those natural barriers: along the roads, in a truck.

Out and About

Some 11,000 game farms and ranches holding hundreds of thousands of deer and elk dot the U.S. and Canada. Besides harvesting the meat, ranchers can sell the antlers—those from elk are marketed as a supplement in vitamin stores ("velvet antler") and as an aphrodisiac in Asia ("velvet Viagra"). To start such farms, ranchers must buy breeding cervids. Somewhere along the line, businesses must have picked up incubating animals from the endemic area. And the interstate trade of cervids continued the spread, west across the Continental Divide and east across the Mississippi River. (These days most states regulate such trade.)

The first farmed cervid to display signs of CWD was an elk that fell ill in 1996 on a ranch in Saskatchewan. By 2001 some 20 ranches reported cases across six states (Colorado, Kansas, Montana, Nebraska, Oklahoma and South Dakota) and one other Canadian province (Alberta). Quick, aggressive measures—namely, killing off the herds—appear to have eliminated the problems on the ranches.

Nevertheless, the transport of incubating cervids may have carried CWD to wild populations in those states and beyond—such as to white-tailed deer in

Wisconsin's eradication zone. But precisely when and how mule deer gave it to white-tailed deer, the most common type in the eastern U.S., is unknown and may never be clear. "By the time these problems are discovered," Miller says, "they have probably been sitting there for decades, which makes it difficult to go back and retrace how things came about." Based on epidemiological models and on Wisconsin's roughly 1.6 percent incidence in the eradication zone, Miller thinks CWD had probably been lurking there since the early 1990s.

Wisconsin's approach makes sense to scientists studying prion diseases. "The idea is to find a fairly small focus and get rid of all the animals in the area," in the hopes of preventing CWD from attaining a permanent hold in the region, Williams says. A rapid spread is possible in Wisconsin because the deer population in the state's southwestern corner is dense: Thomas Givnish, an expert on the ecology of diseases at the University of Wisconsin–Madison, notes that it runs about 50 to 100 deer per square mile, or 10 times that of the endemic area around Fort Collins. "The alternative is to do nothing," Williams observes, and then "you know it's going to be established." By the end of March, Wisconsin hunters had bagged 9,287 deer—which will cut the fall population by 25 percent but will not eliminate CWD, notes state wildlife biologist Tom Howard. A few more seasons of liberal hunting may be needed.

Considering the persistence of prions, Wisconsin may have to live with CWD, as Colorado does. "The disease has been here a long time," Miller comments of CWD around northeastern Colorado. "We can't get rid of it here. We try to get infection rates down so that it can't spread." Miller says that Colorado had hoped to purge CWD through culling. But "we discovered we were 10 to 20 years too late. It was already out there; we didn't realize it." That statement may apply to other states that have found CWD among wild deer, including Illinois and New Mexico.

Venison and Beyond

No one knows whether CWD can pass to humans. A test tube study mixed CWD prions with normal prion proteins from cervids, humans, sheep and cows. The CWD prions had a hard time converting normal human PrP—less than 7 percent of the protein was changed. The downside is that CWD prions converted human PrP about as efficiently as BSE prions do. And because BSE has infected humans, CWD might pose a similar risk. But because beef is far more popular than venison, CWD doesn't present quite the same public health threat.

To see if CWD has already infected people, the Centers for Disease Control and Prevention investigated the deaths of the three young venison eaters who succumbed to sporadic Creutzfeldt-Jakob disease. All were younger than 30 years, which is exceedingly rare in CJD. In fact, through May 31, 2000, just one other U.S. case of sporadic CJD occurred in this age group since surveillance began in 1979.

The first was a 28-year-old cashier, who died in 1997; she had eaten deer and elk as a child, from her father's hunts in Maine. The second was a 30-year-old salesman from Utah who had been hunting regularly since 1985 and who died in 1999. The third was a 27-year-old truck driver from Oklahoma who died in 2000; he had harvested deer at least once a year. Tests of the 1,037 deer and elk taken during the 1999 hunting season from the regions where the victims' meat originated all turned up CWD negative (none of the meat came from the endemic area). The victims' brains showed no unique damage or distinct biochemical signs, as is the case with other prion diseases in humans.

Six other patients (all at least middle-aged) raised suspicions about the CWD risk to humans. Three were outdoorsmen from the Midwest who had participated in wild deer and elk feasts and died in the 1990s. The other cases were reported in April and include two from Washington State who hunted together. Researchers, however, could not find any connection with CWD. And states with CWD have not discovered a higher incidence of Creutzfeldt-Jakob disease.

These observations may seem reassuring, but it is too early to conclude that CWD does not pose a human health hazard. The incubation period of prion diseases may span upward of 40 years, and CWD has been spreading noticeably in only the past 10. The rarity of prion diseases and the low national consumption of deer and elk (compared with beef) make it hard to draw any firm conclusions. Because of the uncertainties with CWD and the fact that animal prion diseases have jumped to humans, the CDC warns against eating food derived from any animal with evidence of a spongiform encephalopathy.

Scientists are still trying to determine if CWD poses a threat to livestock. In an ongoing experiment begun in 1997, Hamir and his colleagues injected brain suspensions from CWD mule deer into the brains of 13 Angus beef calves. Two became ill about two years after inoculation, three others nearly five years after. Hamir began repeating the experiment in November 2002, this time with the brains of CWD white-tailed deer.

Under more natural conditions, bovines have not contracted CWD. Williams has kept cows with infected cervids, and more than five years on, the cows are still healthy. Bovines kept with decomposing CWD carcasses or isolated in pens that once housed CWD animals have also remained free of prion disease. (These reports are good news for pasture-grazing cows, which might find themselves in the company of wild deer.) To see whether CWD might pose a danger when eaten, Williams has begun feeding CWD brain matter to calves. The long incubation of these illnesses, however—BSE incubates for up to eight years—means these experiments must continue for several years.

If U.S. livestock so far seem to be safe from CWD, the same cannot be said of other animals. If an infected deer dies in the forest and nobody is there to see it, plenty of coyotes, bobcats and other carnivores will, and they will gladly scavenge what remains of the wasted carcass. Moreover, during the clinical phase, CWD animals undoubtedly make easier prey. The canine family is evidently immune to prion diseases, but felines can contract them. Transmission studies with mountain lions have begun, and local lions that die for unknown reasons end up on the pathology table, Williams says.

Although many states have uncovered CWD, other states "are looking darn hard," Miller says, but have not found it—among them, Arizona, Kansas, Michigan, Montana, Nevada and New Jersey. Apparently, only pockets of outbreaks exist. Wildlife managers therefore have a fighting chance to keep CWD from gaining a permanent grip throughout the country, so long as control efforts begin promptly. Unfortunately, not all states with CWD are as aggressive as Wisconsin when it comes to surveillance and eradication.

To stop or at least slow the spread of the fatal sickness, extensive culling appears to be the best strategy. One could hope that CWD occurs naturally in deer and that the epidemics will run their course and leave behind CWD-resistant cervids. Some lines of sheep, for instance, are immune to scrapie. But so far all white-tailed and mule deer appear to be uniformly susceptible. "I don't think genetics is going to save us on this," remarks the NIH's Race. Sadly, the only way to save the deer, it seems, is to shoot them.

More to Explore

Risk Analysis of Prion Diseases in Animals. Edited by Corinne I. Lasmézas and David B. Adams. *Scientific and Technical Review*, Vol. 22, No. 1; April 2003.

The Pathological Protein: Mad Cow, Chronic Wasting, and Other Deadly Prion Diseases. Philip Yam. Copernicus Books, 2003. (**www.thepathologicalprotein.com**)

Chronic Wasting Disease Alliance Web site is at **www.cwd-info.org.**

U.S. Department of Agriculture Web site on CWD is at **www.aphis.usda.gov/lpa/issues/cwd/cwd.html.**

About the Author

PHILIP YAM is *Scientific American*'s news editor. This article is adapted from his book, *The Pathological Protein: Mad Cow, Chronic Wasting, and Other Deadly Prion Diseases*, published in June.

7. "Hope in a Vial"

By Carol Ezzell

Will there be an AIDS vaccine anytime soon?

It wasn't supposed to be this hard. When HIV, the virus responsible for AIDS, was first identified in 1984, Margaret M. Heckler, then secretary of the U.S. Department of Health and Human Services, predicted that a vaccine to protect against the scourge would be available within two years. Would that it had been so straightforward.

Roughly 20 years into the pandemic, 40 million people on the planet are infected with HIV, and three million died from it last year (20,000 in North America). Although several potential AIDS vaccines are in clinical tests, so far none has lived up to its early promise. Time and again researchers have obtained tantalizing preliminary results only to run up against a brick wall later. As recently as two years ago, AIDS researchers were saying privately that they doubted whether even a partially protective vaccine would be available in their lifetime.

No stunning breakthroughs have occurred since that time, but a trickle of encouraging data is prompting hope to spring anew in the breasts of even jaded AIDS vaccine hunters. After traveling down blind alleys for more than a decade, they are emerging battered but not beaten, ready to strike out in new directions. "It's an interesting time for AIDS vaccine research," observes Gregg Gonsalves, director of treatment and prevention advocacy for Gay Men's Health Crisis in New York City. "I feel like it's Act Two now."

In the theater, Act One serves to introduce the characters and set the scene; in Act Two, conflict deepens and the real action begins. Act One of AIDS vaccine research debuted HIV, one of the first so-called retroviruses to cause a serious human disease. Unlike most other viruses, retroviruses insinuate their genetic material into that of the body cells they invade, causing the viral genes to become a permanent fixture in the infected cells and in the offspring of those cells. Retroviruses also reproduce rapidly and sloppily, providing ample opportunity for the emergence of mutations that allow HIV to shift its identity and thereby give the immune system or antiretroviral drugs the slip.

Act One also spotlighted HIV's opposition—the body's immune response—which consists of antibodies (Y-shaped molecules that stick to and tag invaders such as viruses for destruction) and cytotoxic, or killer, T cells (white blood cells charged with destroying virus-infected cells). For years after infection, the immune system battles mightily against HIV, pitting millions of new cytotoxic T cells against the billions of virus particles hatched from infected cells every day. In addition, the immune system deploys armies of antibodies targeted at HIV, at least early in the course of HIV infection, although the antibodies prove relatively ineffectual against this particular foe.

As the curtain rises for Act Two, HIV still has the stage. Results from the first large-scale trial of an AIDS vaccine should become available at the end of this year, but few scientists are optimistic about it: a preliminary analysis suggests that it works poorly. Meanwhile controversy surrounds a giant, U.S.-government-sponsored trial of another potential vaccine slated to begin this September in Thailand. But waiting in the wings are several approaches that are causing the AIDS research community to sit up and take notice. The strategies are reviving the debate about whether, to be useful, a vaccine must elicit immune responses that totally prevent HIV from colonizing a person's cells or whether a vaccine that falls somewhat short of that mark could be acceptable. Some scientists see potential value in vaccines that would elicit the kinds of immune responses that kick in soon after a virus establishes a foothold in cells. By constraining viral replication more effectively

---

Overview/AIDS Vaccines

- Final results from the first large-scale test of a possible AIDS vaccine will be available at the end of this year, but few researchers are optimistic it will work.
- Scientists are now aiming to generate potential AIDS vaccines that stimulate both arms of the immune system: killer cells and antibodies.
- There are five main subtypes, or clades, of HIV. Researchers are debating whether it will be important to devise vaccines for a given area based on the predominant clade infecting that area.

than the body's natural responses would, such vaccines, they argue, might at least help prolong the lives of HIV-infected people and delay the onset of the symptomatic, AIDS phase of the disease.

In the early 1990s scientists thought they could figure out the best vaccine strategy for preventing AIDS by studying long-term nonprogressors, people who appeared to have harbored HIV for a decade or more but who hadn't yet fallen ill with AIDS. Sadly, many of the nonprogressors have become ill after all. The key to their relative longevity seems to have been "a weakened virus and/or a strengthened immune system," says John P. Moore of Weill Medical College of Cornell University. In other words, they were lucky enough to have encountered a slow-growing form of HIV at a time when their bodies had the ammunition to keep it at bay.

Not Found in Nature?

AIDS vaccine developers have struggled for decades to find the "correlates of immunity" for HIV—the magic combination of immune responses that, once induced by a vaccine, would protect someone against infection. But they keep coming up empty-handed, which leaves them with no road map to guide them in the search for an AIDS vaccine. "We're trying to elicit an immune response not found in nature," admits Max Essex of the Harvard School of Public Health. As a result, the quest for an AIDS vaccine has been a bit scattershot.

To be proved useful, a candidate AIDS vaccine must successfully pass through three stages of human testing. In phase I, researchers administer the vaccine to dozens of people to assess its safety and to establish an appropriate dose. Phase II involves hundreds of people and looks more closely at the vaccine's immunogenicity, its ability to prompt an immune response. In phase III, the potential vaccine is given to thousands of volunteers who are followed for a long time to see whether it protects them from infection. Phase III trials for any drug tend to be costly and difficult to administer. And the AIDS trials are especially challenging because of an ironic requirement: subjects who receive the vaccine must be counseled extensively on how to reduce their chances of infection. They are told, for instance, to use condoms or, in the case of intravenous drug users, clean needles because HIV is spread through sex or blood-to-blood contact. Yet the study will yield results only if some people don't heed the counseling and become exposed anyway.

The first potential vaccine to have reached phase III consists of gp120, a protein that studs the outer envelope of HIV and that the virus uses to latch onto and infect cells. In theory, at least, the presence of gp120 in the bloodstream should activate the recipient's immune system, causing it to quickly mount an attack targeted to gp120 if HIV later finds its way into the body.

This vaccine, which is produced by VaxGen in Brisbane, Calif.—a spin-off of biotech juggernaut

World AIDS Snapshot

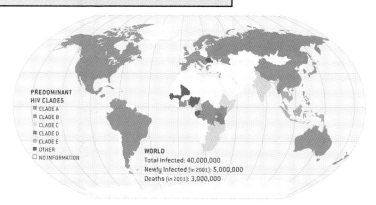

PREDOMINANT
HIV CLADES
- CLADE A
- CLADE B
- CLADE C
- CLADE D
- CLADE E
- OTHER
- NO INFORMATION

WORLD
Total Infected: 40,000,000
Newly Infected (in 2001): 5,000,000
Deaths (in 2001): 3,000,000

1 SUB-SAHARAN AFRICA
Total Infected: 28,100,000
Newly Infected: 3,400,000
Deaths: 2,300,000

2 SOUTH/SOUTHEAST ASIA
Total Infected: 6,100,000
Newly Infected: 800,000
Deaths: 400,000

3 LATIN AMERICA
Total Infected: 1,400,000
Newly Infected: 130,000
Deaths: 80,000

4 EAST ASIA/PACIFIC IS.
Total Infected: 1,000,000
Newly Infected: 270,000
Deaths: 35,000

5 E. EUROPE/C. ASIA
Total Infected: 1,000,000
Newly Infected: 250,000
Deaths: 23,000

6 NORTH AMERICA
Total infected: 940,000
Newly Infected: 45,000
Deaths: 20,000

7 WESTERN EUROPE
Total Infected: 560,000
Newly Infected: 30,000
Deaths: 6,800

8 N. AFRICA/MIDDLE EAST
Total Infected: 440,000
Newly Infected: 80,000
Deaths: 30,000

9 CARIBBEAN
Total Infected: 420,000
Newly Infected: 60,000
Deaths: 30,000

10 AUSTRALIA/NEW ZEALAND
Total Infected: 15,000
Newly Infected: 500
Deaths: 120

Most of the globe's 40 million people infected with HIV live in sub-Saharan Africa and South and Southeast Asia, as reflected in the ranking above, which is based on 2001 data from the Joint United Nations Program on HIV/AIDS. There are five major strains of HIV, which are also called clades. Although more than one clade can usually be found in any given area, the map highlights the predominant clade affecting each region. The boundaries between prevailing clades are not exact; they change frequently.

Genentech in South San Francisco—is being tested in more than 5,400 people (mostly homosexual men) in North America and Europe and in roughly 2,500 intravenous drug users in Southeast Asia. The results from the North American/European trial, which began in 1998, are expected to be announced near the end of this year.

Many AIDS researchers are skeptical of VaxGen's approach because gp120 normally occurs in clumps of three on the surface of the virus, and the company's vaccine employs the molecule in its monomeric, or single-molecule, form. Moreover, vaccines made of just protein generally elicit only an antibody, or humoral, response, without greatly stimulating the cellular arm of the immune system, the part that includes activity by cytotoxic T cells. A growing contingent of investigators suspect that an antibody response alone is not sufficient; a strong cellular response must also be elicited to prevent AIDS.

Indeed, the early findings do not seem encouraging. Last October an independent data-monitoring panel did a preliminary analysis of the results of the North American/European data. Although the panel conducted the analysis primarily to ascertain that the vaccine was causing no dangerous side effects in the volunteers, the reviewers were empowered to recommend halting the trial early if the vaccine appeared to be working. They did not.

For its part, VaxGen asserts that it will seek U.S. Food and Drug Administration approval to sell the vaccine even if the phase III trials show that it reduces a person's likelihood of infection by as little as 30 percent. Company president and co-founder Donald P. Francis points out that the first polio vaccine, developed by Jonas Salk in 1954, was only 60 percent effective, yet it slashed the incidence of polio in the U.S. quickly and dramatically.

This approach could backfire, though, if people who receive a partially effective AIDS vaccine believe they are then protected from infection and can engage in risky behaviors. Karen M. Kuntz and Elizabeth Bogard of the Harvard School of Public Health have constructed a computer model simulating the effects of such a vaccine in a group of injection drug users in Thailand. According to their model, a 30 percent effective vaccine would not slow the spread of AIDS in a community if 90 percent of the people who received it went back to sharing needles or using dirty needles. They found that such reversion to risky behavior would not wash out the public health benefit if a vaccine were at least 75 percent effective.

The controversial study set to begin in Thailand is also a large-scale phase III trial, involving nearly 16,000 people. It combines the VaxGen vaccine with a canarypox virus into which scientists have stitched genes that encode gp120 as well as two other proteins—one that makes up the HIV core and one that allows it to reproduce. Because this genetically engineered canarypox virus (made by Aventis Pasteur, headquartered in Lyons, France) enters cells and causes them to display fragments of HIV on their surface, it stimulates the cellular arm of the immune system.

Political wrangling and questions over its scientific value have slowed widespread testing of the gp120/canarypox vaccine. Initially the National Institute of Allergy and Infectious Diseases (NIAID) and the U.S. Department of Defense were scheduled to conduct

One AIDS Vaccine Strategy

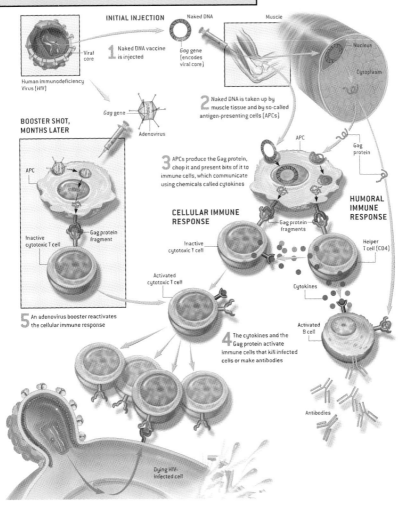

INITIAL INJECTION Naked DNA | Muscle

1 Naked DNA vaccine is injected

Viral core

Gag gene (encodes viral core)

Human immunodeficiency Virus (HIV)

Nucleus

Cytoplasm

BOOSTER SHOT, MONTHS LATER

Gag gene

Adenovirus

2 Naked DNA is taken up by muscle tissue and by so-called antigen-presenting cells (APCs)

APC

Gag protein

APC

3 APCs produce the Gag protein, chop it and present bits of it to immune cells, which communicate using chemicals called cytokines

CELLULAR IMMUNE RESPONSE

HUMORAL IMMUNE RESPONSE

Gag protein fragments

Inactive cytotoxic T cell

Gag protein fragment

Inactive cytotoxic T cell

Helper T cell (CD4)

Activated cytotoxic T cell

Cytokines

5 An adenovirus booster reactivates the cellular immune response

Activated B cell

4 The cytokines and the Gag protein activate immune cells that kill infected cells or make antibodies

Antibodies

Dying HIV-infected cell

A vaccine approach being pioneered by Merck involves an initial injection of a naked DNA vaccine followed months later by a booster shot of crippled, genetically altered adenovirus particles. Both are designed to elicit an immune response targeted to the HIV core protein, Gag, and to primarily arouse the cellular arm of the immune system—the one that uses cytotoxic T cells to destroy virus-infected cells. The naked DNA vaccine also results in the production of antibody molecules against Gag, but such antibodies are not very useful in fighting HIV.

essentially duplicate trials of the vaccine. But NIAID pulled the plug on its trial after an examination of the data from a phase II study showed that fewer than 30 percent of the volunteers generated cytotoxic T cells against HIV. And in a bureaucratic twist, this past January the White House transferred the budget for the Defense Department trial over to NIAID as part of an effort to streamline AIDS research.

Peggy Johnston, assistant director of AIDS vaccines for NIAID, says she expects there will be a trial of the vaccine but emphasizes that "it will be a Thai trial; we won't have any [NIAID] people there on the ground running things."

Critics cite these machinations as a case study of politics getting in the way of progress against AIDS. "There's little science involved" in the trial, claims one skeptic, who wonders why the Thais aren't asking, "'If it's not good enough for America, how come it's good enough for us?'" Others point out that the trial, which was conceived by the Defense Department, will answer only the question of whether the vaccine works; it won't collect any data that scientists could use to explain its potential failure.

Partial Protection

Into this scene comes Merck, which is completing separate phase I trials of two different vaccine candidates that it has begun to test together. In February, Emilio A. Emini, Merck's senior vice president for vaccine research, wowed scientists attending the Ninth Conference on Retroviruses and Opportunistic Infections in Seattle with the company's initial data from the two trials.

The first trial is investigating a potential vaccine composed of only the HIV gag gene, which encodes the virus's core protein. It is administered as a so-called naked DNA vaccine, consisting solely of DNA. Cells take up the gene and use it as a blueprint for making the viral protein, which in turn stimulates a mild (and probably unhelpful) humoral response and a more robust cellular response [see "One AIDS Vaccine Strategy" illustration]. Emini and his colleagues reported that 42 percent of volunteers who received the highest dose of the naked DNA vaccine raised cytotoxic T cells capable of attacking HIV-infected cells.

The second trial employs the HIV gag gene spliced into a crippled adenovirus, the class responsible for many common colds. This altered adenovirus ferries the gag gene into cells, which then make the HIV core protein and elicit an immune response targeted to that protein. Emini told the conference that between 44 and 67 percent of people who received injections of the adenovirus-based vaccine generated a cellular immune response that varied in intensity according to the size of the dose the subjects received and how long ago they got their shots.

Merck is now beginning to test a combination of the DNA and adenovirus approaches because Emini predicts that the vaccines will work best when administered as part of the same regimen. "The concept," he says, "is not that the DNA vaccine will be a good vaccine on its own, but that it may work as a primer of the immune system," to be followed months later by a booster shot of the adenovirus vaccine. A possible stumbling block is that most people have had colds caused by adenoviruses. Accordingly, the immune systems of such individuals would already have an arsenal in place that could wipe out the adenovirus vaccine before it had a chance to deliver its payload of HIV genes and stimulate AIDS immunity. Increasing the dose of the adenovirus vaccine could get around this obstacle.

Emini says he and his co-workers are emphasizing cellular immunity in part because of the disappointing results so far with vaccines designed to engender humoral responses. "Antibodies continue to be a problem," he admits. "There are a handful of reasonably potent antibodies isolated from HIV-infected people, but we haven't figured out how to raise those antibodies using a vaccine."

Lawrence Corey of the Fred Hutchinson Cancer Research Center in Seattle agrees: "You'd like to have both [a cellular and an antibody response], but the greatest progress has been in eliciting a cellular response," says Corey, who is also principal investigator of the federally funded HIV Vaccine Trials Network.

Antibodies are important, too, because they are the immune system's first line of defense and are thought to be the key to preventing viruses from ever contacting the cells they infect. Corey says that vaccines that are designed primarily to evoke cellular immunity (as are Merck's) are not likely to prevent infection but should give someone a head start in combating the virus if he or she does become infected. "Instead of progressing to AIDS in eight years, you progress in 25 years," he predicts. But, Corey adds, it is unclear whether a vaccine that only slowed disease progression would stem the AIDS pandemic, because people would still be able to spread the infection to others despite having less virus in their bloodstream.

Finding a way to induce the production of antibodies able to neutralize HIV has been hard slogging for several reasons. For one, the virus's shape-shifting ways allow it to stay one step ahead of the immune response. "The thing that distinguishes HIV from all other human viruses is its ability to mutate so fast," Essex says. "By the time you make a neutralizing antibody [against HIV], it is only against the virus that was in you a month ago."

According to many scientists, vaccines using a logical molecule, gp120—the protein the virus uses to invade immune cells, as discussed above—haven't worked, probably because the antibodies that such vaccines elicit bind to the wrong part of the molecule. Gp120 shields the precise binding site it uses to latch onto CD4, its docking site on immune cells, until the last nanosecond, when it snaps open like a jackknife. One way to get around this problem, suggested in a paper published in *Science* three years ago by

Jack H. Nunberg of the University of Montana and his colleagues, would be to make vaccines of gp120 molecules that have previously been exposed to CD4 and therefore have already sprung open. But those results have been "difficult to replicate," according to Corey, making researchers pessimistic about the approach.

Another possible hurdle to getting an AIDS vaccine that elicits effective anti-HIV antibodies is the variety of HIV subtypes, or clades, that affect different areas of the world. There are five major clades, designated A through E [see "World AIDS Snapshot" illustration]. Although clade B is the predominant strain in North America and Europe, most of sub-Saharan Africa—the hardest-hit region of the globe—has clade C. The ones primarily responsible for AIDS in South and Southeast Asia—the second biggest AIDS hot spot—are clades B, C and E.

Several studies indicate that antibodies that recognize AIDS viruses from one clade might not bind to viruses from other clades, suggesting that a vaccine made from the strain found in the U.S. might not protect people in South Africa, for example. But scientists disagree about the significance of clade differences and whether only strains that match the most prevalent clade in a given area can be tested in countries there. Essex, who is gearing up to lead phase I tests of a clade C–based vaccine in Botswana later this year, argues that unless researchers are sure that a vaccine designed against one clade can cross-react with viruses from another, they must stick to testing vaccines that use the clade prevalent in the populations being studied. Cross-reactivity could occur under ideal circumstances, but, he says, "unless we know that, it's important for us to use subtype-specific vaccines."

Using the corresponding clade also avoids the appearance that people in developing countries are being used as guinea pigs for testing a vaccine that is designed to work only in the U.S. or Europe. VaxGen's tests in Thailand are based on a combination of clades B and E, and in April the International AIDS Vaccine Initiative expanded tests of a clade A–derived vaccine in Kenya, where clade A is found.

But in January, Malegapuru William Makgoba and Nandipha Solomon of the Medical Research Council of South Africa, together with Timothy Johan Paul Tucker of the South African AIDS Vaccine Initiative, wrote in the *British Medical Journal* that the relevance of HIV subtypes "remains unresolved." They assert that clades "have assumed a political and national importance, which could interfere with important international trials of efficacy."

Early data from the Merck vaccine trials suggest that clade differences blur when it comes to cellular immunity. At the retrovirus conference in February, Emini reported that killer cells from 10 of 13 people who received a vaccine based on clade B also reacted in laboratory tests to viral proteins from clade A or C viruses. "There is a potential for a substantial cross-clade response" in cellular immunity, he says, "but that's not going to hold true for antibodies." Corey concurs that clade variation "is likely to play much, much less of a role" for killer cells than for antibodies because most cytotoxic T cells recognize parts of HIV that are the same from clade to clade.

Johnston of NIAID theorizes that one answer would be to use all five major clades in every vaccine. Chiron in Emeryville, Calif., is developing a multi-clade vaccine, which is in early clinical trials. Such an approach could be overkill, however, Johnston says. It could be that proteins from only one clade would be recognized "and the other proteins would be wasted," she warns.

Whatever the outcome on the clade question, Moore of Weill Medical College says he and fellow researchers are more hopeful than they were a few years ago about their eventual ability to devise an AIDS vaccine that would elicit both killer cells and antibodies. "The problem is not impossible," he says, "just extremely difficult."

More to Explore

HIV Vaccine Efforts Inch Forward. Brian Vastag in *Journal of the American Medical Association*, Vol. 286, No. 15, pages 1826–1828; October 17, 2001.
For an overview of AIDS vaccine research, including the status of U.S.-funded AIDS clinical trials, visit **www.niaid.nih.gov/daids/vaccine/default.htm.**

A global perspective on the AIDS pandemic and the
need for a vaccine can be found at the International
AIDS Vaccine Initiative Web site: **www.iavi.org**
Joint United Nations Program on HIV/AIDS:
www.unaids.org

About the Author

CAROL EZZELL is a staff editor and writer.

Web Sites

Due to the changing nature of Internet links, Rosen Publishing has developed an online list of Web sites related to the subject of this book. This site is updated regularly. Please use this link to access the list:

http://www.rosenlinks.com/saces/gewa

For Further Reading

Brown, Jack. *Don't Touch That Doorknob! How Germs Can Zap You and How You Can Zap Back.* New York, NY: Grand Central Publishing, 2001.

Gehlbach, Stephen H. *American Plagues: Lessons from Our Battles with Disease.* New York, NY: McGraw-Hill, 2004.

Johnson, Steven. *The Ghost Map.* New York, NY: Riverhead, 2006.

Nardo, Don. *Germs* (Great Medical Discoveries). New York, NY: Lucent Books, 2003.

Waller, John. *The Discovery of the Germ: Twenty Years That Transformed the Way We Think About Disease.* New York, NY: Columbia University Press, 2003.

INDEX